The State, Law and Religion

ALAN WATSON

The State, Law and Religion

PAGAN ROME

The University of Georgia Press

Athens and London

Paperback edition, 2012
© 1992 by the University of Georgia Press
Athens, Georgia 30602
www.ugapress.org
All rights reserved
Set in Times Roman with Trajanus display by
Tseng Information System, Inc.
Printed digitally in the United States of America

The Library of Congress has cataloged the hardcover edition of
this book as follows:
Watson, Alan.
The state, law, and religion : pagan Rome / Alan Watson.
xv 136 p. ; 24 cm.
Includes bibliographical references and index.
ISBN 0-8203-1387-4 (alk. paper)
1. Religion and law—Rome. 2. Roman law. 3. Religion and state—
Rome. 4. Rome—Religion. I. Title.
KJA3060 .W37   1992
340.5'4—dc20   91-14391

Paperback ISBN-13: 978-0-8203-4118-7
ISBN-10: 0-8203-4118-5

British Library Cataloging-in-Publication Data available

FOR SARAH EMANUEL

Contents

Preface *ix*

Acknowledgments *xi*

List of Abbreviations *xiii*

Introduction *1*

1   Prolegomena on Roman Religion *4*
2   The Twelve Tables: Contents *14*
3   The Twelve Tables: The Public/Private Law Distinction *21*
4   Formalism in Religion and Law *30*
5   *Votum* and *Stipulatio* *39*
6   The Oath in Private Law *44*
7   The Pontiffs and the Family *51*
8   Religion and Property *55*
9   State Religion and Alien Religion *58*
10 The Pontiffs and Legal Development *63*
11 The Paradox Resolved *73*
12 The *Leges Regiae* *87*

Appendix *91*

Notes *95*

Index of Texts *131*

Preface

It is a curious fact that no one has written a comprehensive account of the interaction of law and religion in ancient Rome.[1] Law and religion are among the most powerful organized forces in society; hence a knowledge of how they interact, or fail to interact, is vital for understanding a people's moral, political, and social attitudes. This is especially true when the religion is a state or official religion, and it should be particularly the case for ancient Rome. Roman law, after all, was the most innovative legal system in the Western world, and it has been the most influential. In the later republic, at least until the latter part of the second century B.C., the Romans regarded themselves, and were regarded by others, as the most religious people in the world.[2] The empire saw the legalized persecution of the Christians. The eventual adoption of Christianity as the state religion shaped much of later history.

My present subject is the interaction of law and religion during the republic and empire until Christianity was legally recognized and encouraged by Constantine and subsequently adopted as the state religion. Among the questions one might ask are, How does state organized religion affect the general development of law? What is the impact of religious doctrines on the substance of law? What use is made of religion to support law? What legal protection is given to religion? What are the legal forms used for the persecution of dangerous religions?

For me, the most important and interesting issue has turned out to be the impact of the state religion on legal development, and the implications of this for the nature of Roman law. This impact was not always direct, but the growth of the law cannot rightly be understood without an awareness of the nature of Roman state religion. Legal scholars—and Roman political historians, too—should not relegate knowledge of religion to a footnote in the mind.[3] Indeed, at the heart of this book is an apparent paradox. Roman private law received its distinctive characteristics during the republic and that law is remarkably secular. Yet the Romans of the day were renowned for their attachment to religion, and the development of the law itself was largely under the control of the priests, the pontifices, or pontiffs. How could that be? In this book I strive to provide the answer.

I have not directly addressed the very controverted issue of the accuracy of the sources, such as Livy, for very early Rome. I am well aware of the danger of attributing credibility to them, but the fact is, as I have argued in the past, Livy, who clearly does not have a deep understanding of law, almost always presents a plausible account of archaic institutions.[4] I hope the coherence of this volume will strengthen the feeling of plausibility.

It is my hope that this study will be followed by a volume that concerns the period from Constantine onward. By the time Constantine made Christianity an official Roman religion, the system of Roman private law was fully developed and firmly in place. Yet the Christian Fathers had their own views on what the law should be. In the next volume I will examine Christian doctrines and elucidate their impact on pagan Roman law.

Acknowledgments

This book was written at the University of Georgia Law School, and I wish to thank my colleagues there for their encouragement. The staff of the Law School Library and of the University Library were unfailingly helpful. Karen Bramlett dealt most cheerfully and efficiently with numerous drafts. Several friends read the whole manuscript at various stages and greatly helped me with their criticisms: John Cairns, Calum Carmichael, Robert Curtis, Paul Heald, Peter Krause, Olivia Robinson, Jim Whitman, and Elise Zoli. Jerzy Linderski, above all, who read the typescript for the University of Georgia Press, put his unique combination of knowledge of Roman religion, law, and history at my disposal.

My biggest debt is to my teacher, David Daube, who was constantly in my thoughts while I was working. His influence on me is pervasive. The studies of ancient law and religion, by no means restricted to Rome, are peculiarly his own, and without the training I received from him I could not have embarked on this book. May the results not disappoint him.

Abbreviations

Bruns, *Fontes*	C.G. Bruns, *Fontes Iuris Romani*, 7th ed., O. Gradenwitz (Tübingen, 1909).
C.A.H. 7.2	*The Cambridge Ancient History*, vol. 7, book 2, *The Rise of Rome to 200 B.C.*, 2d ed., F. W. Walbank, A. E. Astin, M. W. Frederiksen, and R. M. Ogilvie (Cambridge, 1989).
C.I.L.	*Corpus Inscriptionum Latinarum* (Berlin, 1863–).
D.	The *Digest* of Justinian.
Der Kleine Pauly 1–5	*Der Kleine Pauly: Lexikon der Antike*, vols. 1–5, ed. K. Ziegler and W. Southeimer (Munich, 1975).
Dumézil, *Religion* 1, 2	G. Dumézil, *Archaic Roman Religion*, vols. 1 and 2 (Chicago, 1970).
FIRA 1	*Fontes Iuris Romani Antejustiniani*, vol. 1, 2d ed., ed. S. Riccobono (Florence, 1941).
G.	The *Institutes* of Gaius.
J.	The *Institutes* of Justinian.
Jolowicz and Nicholas, *Introduction*	H. F. Jolowicz and B. Nicholas, *Historical Introduction to the Study of Roman Law*, 3d ed. (Cambridge, 1972).
Kaser, *Privatrecht* 1	M. Kaser, *Das römische Privatrecht*, vol. 1, 2d ed. (Munich, 1971).
Kaser, *Zivilprozessrecht*	M. Kaser, *Das römische Zivilprozessrecht* (Munich, 1966).
Kunkel, *Herkunft*	W. Kunkel, *Herkunft and soziale Stellung der römischen Juristen*, 2d ed. (Graz, 1967).

Abbreviations

Latte, *Religionsgeschichte* — K. Latte, *Römische Religionsgeschichte*, 2d ed. (Munich, 1967).

Lenel, *Edictum* — Otto Lenel, *Das Edictum perpetuum*, 3d ed. (Leipzig, 1927).

Liebeschuetz, *Continuity* — J. H. W. G. Liebeschuetz, *Continuity and Change in Roman Religion* (Oxford, 1979).

LQR — *Law Quarterly Review*.

Michels, *Calendar* — A. K. Michels, *The Calendar of the Roman Republic* (Princeton, 1967).

Mitchell, *Patricians and Plebians* — R. E. Mitchell, *Patricians and Plebians: The Origins of the Roman State* (Ithaca, 1990).

Mommsen, *Staatsrecht*, 1, 2, 3 — T. Mommsen, *Römisches Staatsrecht*, vols. 1 and 2, 3rd ed. (Leipzig, 1887); vol. 3, 1st ed. (Leipzig, 1888).

Nicolet, *World of the Citizen* — C. Nicolet, *The World of the Citizen in Republican Rome* (Berkeley, 1980).

RIDA — *Revue Internationale des Droits de l'Antiquité*.

Rotondi, *Leges publicae* — G. Rotondi, *Leges publicae populi romani* (Milan, 1912).

Schulz, *Legal Science* — F. Schulz, *History of Roman Legal Science* (Oxford, 1946).

Talamanca, *Lineamenti* — M. Talamanca, et al., *Lineamenti di storia del diritto romano*, 2d ed. (Milan, 1989).

Thomas, *Textbook* — J. A. C. Thomas, *Textbook of Roman Law* (Amsterdam, 1976).

T.v.R. — *Tijdschrift voor Rechtsgeschiedenis*.

Wardman, *Religion* — A. Wardman, *Religion and Statecraft among the Romans* (Baltimore, 1982).

Watson, *Evolution of Law* — Alan Watson, *The Evolution of Law* (Baltimore, 1985).

Watson, *Law Making* — Alan Watson, *Law Making in the Later Roman Republic* (Oxford, 1974).

Watson, *XII Tables*	Alan Watson, *Rome of the XII Tables* (Princeton, 1975).
Wieacker, *Rechtsgeschichte*	F. Wieacker, *Römische Rechtsgeschichte*, vol. 1 (Munich, 1988).
Wissowa, *Religion und Kultus*	G. Wissowa, *Religion und Kultus der Römer*, 2d ed. (Leipzig, 1912).
ZSS	*Zeitschrift der Savigny-Stiftung (romanistische Abteilung)*.

Introduction

The development of Roman private law as it appears in this book is so different from standard accounts that it is appropriate at the beginning to set out the main theses about law in a simplified form, quite independently of the course of argument in the main body of the book.

The most prominent—but not necessarily the most important—issue is why Roman law is so remarkably secular, especially since the Romans were the most religious people of the time, and the interpretation of civil law was long the preserve of the College of Pontiffs. The explanation lies above all in the history of the Twelve Tables, the codification of the mid-fifth century B.C.

Not long after the expulsion of the last Roman king in 509 B.C., trouble broke out between the patricians, the aristocratic top rank of society, and the great bulk of Roman citizenry, the plebeians. According to the ancient sources, the plebeians' main demands were for laws establishing equality among the citizens, and laws delineating and limiting the powers of the top officials of the state. After considerable struggle, the senate decreed that ten men, all of whom had to be patricians, were to prepare a body of law. The result was the Twelve Tables.

The patrician lawmakers did produce a body of law that was extremely egalitarian, with no differences in law between one man and another on account of wealth or social standing. This has to be seen as intentional. But in spite of appearances, the Twelve Tables were a defeat for the plebeians, with lasting consequences. The Twelve Tables dealt only with those matters with regard to which the patrician legislators were willing to grant equality between patrician and plebeian, and which, moreover, they regarded as appropriate for the attention of plebeians. Thus, public law was entirely omitted, and the plebeians did not achieve their demand of having the powers of the consuls delimited. In public law gross inequalities continued between one class of citizens and another, and in the assemblies of the people wealth dominated voting rights— and it was an assembly that elected the leading state officials. Again, astonishingly perhaps, until the late second century B.C. only senators could be judges even in civil cases, and thereafter only members of the equestrian order could be appointed as such. Roman public law was never to be the object of comprehensive legislation and did not develop by interpretation to the extent that private law did. Sacred law was omitted from the Twelve Tables as being not the business of plebeians, since only patricians could be priests of the state religion. The argument here is not that religious elements were cut out of the provisions on private law, but the rules that predominantly concerned religious law were not set out in the code.

Thus came about, as the result of particular circumstances, the famous division between public and private law that is with us today.

The job of interpreting the Twelve Tables was given to one of the main colleges of priests, the College of Pontiffs. This was an astute move on the part of the patricians, since the pontiffs (who were part-time priests) not only had to be patricians themselves but were men of distinguished public service with an established, known, record.[1] Moreover, they already had the responsibility of interpreting sacred law. The College of Pontiffs appointed one pontifex, or pontiff, per year to interpret the Twelve Tables.

In keeping with the Roman view that the business of the state religion was to maintain the right relations between the gods and humans (especially public officials and the state), the pontiffs did not carry the characteristics of Roman religion over to private law, which concerned relations between private individuals. But, probably unconsciously, they used for interpreting private law the same approaches that they used for sacred law. Hence, a decision could not be reached on the basis that it was economically efficient or benevolent or useful but primarily on internal, legal, grounds. The resulting enclosed, legalistic form of reasoning toward a decision is not obviously the most appropriate for private law. Decisions are not, in appearance at least, result oriented, and law was on its way to becoming autonomous from the interests of society.

The state monopoly of interpreting civil law, now in the hands of one individual pontiff, meant that interpretation of the law was a worthy task for a gentleman. That view continued even after the College of Pontiffs both ceased to be the preserve of patricians and also lost its monopoly of interpretation. The high social prestige of the jurists, and the prediliction of the Roman upper class for giving legal opinions, resulted from this early situation. So also did the state's willingness to allow private individuals to develop the law by interpretation. It is this that largely explains the high level of development of Roman private law, despite the state's failure to produce much legislation.

But a further consequence of this early pontifical monopoly of interpretation was that it closed the door to development by custom and even by judicial decision. This increased the extent of law's autonomy from society.

The main characteristics of developed Roman law thus resulted in large measure from a particular political conflict in the mid-fifth century B.C. Though we need not here take the argument further, without these characteristics there could not have occurred the all-important Reception of Roman law.

1 Prolegomena on Roman Religion

Scholars are generally agreed on the broad outline of law in the Roman republic. There is less agreement, however, on the nature of Roman religion.[1] The aim, therefore, in this first chapter is to present a sketch of the state religion that is plausible, self-consistent, and true to the sources. No claim is made that other outlines may not also be plausible. But subsequent chapters will reveal facets of the interaction of law and religion which, I believe, will make convincing the sketch given here.

When the book was begun, it seemed proper to start with the better known and proceed to the less well known; hence in this case, from law to religion. And in what follows, significant and surprising features in the law will help to explain Roman religion.[2] The book has turned out to be primarily, however, an account of the development of Roman private law which is radically different from that usually presented. Accordingly, a preliminary account of Roman religion is needed to provide a framework.[3]

Like the Latin language, Roman state religion was of Indo-European origin.[4] Just as Latin shares morphology and linguistic roots with Sanskrit, Greek, Celtic, and other Indo-European languages, so Roman state religion shares elements such as the archaic triad of deities—in Rome, Jupiter, Mars, and Quirinus—with other peoples of Indo-European origin. But the fate of Indo-European religion, like language, differed from place to place. As rich in myths as Indo-European religion was,[5] this richness was much enhanced in Greece. In Vedic India, religion was to reach new heights of mysticism. But among the Roman people official religion lost its mythology. The major deities had no histories and no adventures. The gods became depersonalized. The bareness in the religion as it appears in historical times is not primitive or original but acquired.[6] The intervention of the gods in human affairs was essentially discontinuous.[7] At least in appearance, Roman state religion lost its vitality.[8]

Not only that, but Roman state religion was not concerned with the question of how its devotees should lead the moral life. Hostile witness as he is, Augustine poses the relevant question why it is that the Roman gods did not lay down laws to aid their worshippers to lead the good life. "It would certainly appear proper that the care shown by the worshippers for the gods' rites be matched by the gods' concern for their behavior." [9]

But it remained the official religion. There is nothing surprising in this. Tradition dies very hard, and there is nothing so traditional as religion.[10] This is not to suggest that changes in official religion did not occur—many did, even such important renewals as the introduction of the Capitoline triad, Jupiter, Juno, and Minerva, in Etruscan times.[11] Again, the deities, Ceres, Liber, and Libera were introduced from Magna Graecia in 493 B.C., with a temple at the end of the Campus Martius near the Aventine.[12] Nor should we see in the perseverance of this seemingly sterile state religion a cynicism, an absence of belief in the existence of the gods.

Rather, state religion became restricted to a particular context.[13] It became a matter of keeping man—especially man in his public function—in proper contact with the gods. The functions of the priests were to ensure that ceremonies were correctly and formalistically carried out in every detail. They had to ensure, for example, that meetings of the senate or comitia were opened with prayers said according to the fixed and rigid formulas. They had to see to it that the days on which such assemblies met or on which the praetor made pronouncements were auspicious. They were, in this way, responsible for the calendar. They also had to make sure that each sacrifice was carried out precisely in the way acceptable to the gods. They dictated to state officials what was religiously proper in the conduct of business, including the business of war. State religion was very important, but it became confined to its context. The main functions of the priests became, from a modern perspective, legal.[14]

Beneath the highest deities—not in the hierarchical sense, but in terms of importance—were many others, and they, above all, reveal the fundamentally peasant nature of Roman religion. One should not, however, draw a sharp distinction between the "official religion" and the "folk religion"—as distinct from unauthorized "foreign cults"—since both had state recognition, but the main concern here is with the leading gods and goddesses.[15] The divine, however, was to be found everywhere.[16]

There were many classes of priests, but for convenience we may very largely restrict our consideration to the most important of the four great colleges of priests, the College of Pontiffs.[17] This body contained the pontiffs (including the *pontifex maximus*), the *rex sacrorum,* and the flamines (three *maiores* and twelve *minores*); closely associated with it were the vestal virgins (of whom there were six). Of these, the pontiffs in the narrow sense were during the regal period the advisors (*consilium*) of the king for matters relating to the gods.[18] Thereafter the College of Pontiffs performed that function for the senate, which itself developed from what had also been the king's advisory body.[19] Since the *regia*, "royal palace," was the center of religious activities during the republic and it was here that the pontiffs held their deliberations, it would appear that after the fall of the monarchy the pontiffs were considered to replace the king to some extent in religious matters.[20] The *rex sacrorum* performed the religious functions for which the king had been responsible in his own person.[21] There is no indication that the *rex sacrorum* was regarded as having magical powers and he was not surrounded by taboos as the flamines were.[22] The flamines, in contrast to the pontiffs in the narrow sense, were the priests for a particular deity, the three *flamines maiores* being in order, respectively, Dialis, Martialis, Quirinalis.[23]

The pontiffs had various functions which can be distinguished. First, they gave instructions, above all to officials, for the proper performance of sacral acts such as the dedication of a temple, and they preserved the appropriate oral formulas. They oversaw activities in the assembly known as the *comitia calata*. They kept the calendar which set out the days on which the courts could sit, votes could be taken, sacrifices could be made, and on which the senate could issue valid *decreta*.[24] They had also been the guardians of the general pronouncements of the kings, whether on sacral or on other matters. The *pontifex maximus* had disciplinary jurisdiction over the vestal virgins.[25] These matters—apart from the last—will appear in later chapters. Here we need deal only with their remaining function, their giving of *responsa*.[26] They might deliver their opinion on the religious "legality" of a course of action upon request by the senate or by a magistrate. The opinion might relate to a past event, in which case the *responsum* might be termed a judicial pronouncement.[27] It is in this sense that Festus claims: "He is called the *pontifex maximus* because he is the chief [*maximus*] judge of matters that appertain to religion and the sacred, and is the avenger of stubbornness of private individuals and of magistrates."[28] The *pontifex maximus* was the spokesman for the College of Pontiffs.[29] But the text of Festus must not mislead: no action was taken by the pontiffs on their *responsum*. It was declaratory only, to set out the proper conduct of men to gods, and it was not followed by execution of judgment. Nor could it be. It was not normally part of the College of Pontiffs' functions to examine the facts.[30] They responded only to the terms of the facts proposed to them. Thus, a standard decree might contain words such as: *si ea ita sunt que libelo contenentur*, "If the facts are those that are contained in the petition."[31] The decree of the pontiffs on the issue whether Cicero's house had been properly consecrated as a temple—by an enemy, in order to deprive him of it—ran (as reported by him): "Si neque populi iussu neque plebis scitu is, qui se dedicasse diceret, nominatim ei rei praefectus esset neque populi iussu aut plebis scitu id facere iussus esset, videri posse sine religione eam partem arcae mihi restitui" (If the person claiming to have dedicated had not been appointed by name either by order of the people or by a decree of the plebs, and if he had not been commanded to do so by an order of the people or decree of the plebs, then it appeared that that part of the site might be restored to me without sacrilege.)[32] In this instance we have the speech delivered by Cicero before the pontiffs.[33] The pontiffs heard the alleged facts, but they used their information only to set the appropriate legal parameters. They made no finding of fact. The decree just quoted leaves unresolved the issue of fact. Cicero, indeed, reports that he was immediately congratulated when the decree was issued, but then someone got up and claimed that the decree was actually against Cicero, who was trying to seize the temple of Liberty by force.[34]

Again, the pontiffs might issue a *responsum* when asked whether a contemplated sacred act was permitted. This may be regarded as an instance of cautelary jurisprudence.[35] Two episodes reported by Livy are instructive. In 203 B.C. one of the consuls set out to the army in Lucania. The other consul, Marcellus, was delayed:

> Religious scruples, one after the other, as they were impressed upon his mind, detained Marcellus. One of them was that, although he had vowed a temple to Honor and Valor at Clastidium in the Gallic war, its dedication was hindered by the pontiffs, [8.] because they denied that one chapel could be properly dedicated to more than one god because, if it should be struck by lightning or some portent should occur in it, expiation would be difficult [9.] because it would be impossible to know to which god sacrifice should be made: for, except to certain deities, one sacrifice could not be offered to two.[36]

In Livy, the arguments for the pontiffs' stance are given in indirect speech: that is, Livy is (ostensibly) not providing his own explanation but giving the reasoning expressed by the priests. Thus, the pontiffs are giving not only the decision but the reasons for it. Of course, Livy may well not be historically accurate but that is a matter of little significance. It is enough that for Livy it was plausible that the pontiffs might give reasons of this kind for their decision.

The other episode is from 200 B.C.:

While the consuls levied troops and proposed what was needed for the war, the state, always concerned with religion, especially at the beginning of new wars, [6.] having held thanksgivings and offered prayers at all the seats of the gods, so that nothing should be passed over that had been done before, ordered the consul to whom the province of Macedonia had been allotted, to vow games and a gift to Jupiter. [7.] Licinius, the *pontifex maximus*, was responsible for a delay because he claimed it was not permitted to make a vow of an indefinite sum of money. He said a vow should be made for a fixed sum because this money could not be used for war and should at once be set aside and not mixed with other money. If this were to occur, the vow could not properly be carried out. [8.] Although the consul was moved by both the issue and its author, he was nonetheless directed to consult the College of Pontiffs if a vow of an indeterminate sum of money could properly be made. [9.] The pontiffs decreed that it could be done and was even more correct. [10.] The consul, at the dictation of the *pontifex maximus*, vowed in the same words in which previously the vows for the quinquennial games were made, except that he promised games and a gift of an amount to be determined by the senate when the vow was paid. The great games had eight times previously been vowed for definite sums. These were the first for an indefinite sum.[37]

This time, the initial opinion of the *pontifex maximus* is backed by reasons. Again, Livy gives them in indirect speech, hence again as the reasons of the *pontifex maximus*. And they are strikingly legalistic and formalistic.[38] The passage also indicates that an opinion of a pontiff might be regarded as weighty because of the authority of the respondent, whether this was because of his status or of his perceived ability.

Equally legalistic and formalistic is an opinion of another pontiff, who was consul in 142 B.C.: "But the pontiff, Fabius Maximus Servilianus, says in his twelfth book that one must not on a black day [*dies ater*] make the sacrifice in honor of someone who has died, because one must in this case begin also by invoking Janus and Jupiter, and one must not name them on a black day." [39]

But reasons need not be given for the *responsum*. Thus, an inscription found near Tarracina, from the entrance to a tomb: "To the gods of the dead. The College of Pontiffs decreed, if the facts are those that are contained in the petition, that it is proper to permit the girl about whom the question is raised, to be taken from the shrine and again placed according to the precept, and the inscription to be restored to its previous condition with care being first taken to make expiation with a black sheep." [40] Probably this decree, concerning the reburial of a girl and the restoration of the tomb's inscription, was issued at the request of an individual. Another inscription from Rome reads: "Aelius

Dignus, Paccius Charito and associates possess this tomb surrounded by a wall, with all its rights, on the authority and by the judgment of the pontiffs."[41]

Just as books were written on private law, so were they on pontifical, augural, and sacred law. There were experts on pontifical, augural, and sacred law as there were on private law.[42]

The pontiffs did not act in the name of a particular deity. Rather they were public officials charged with the duty of keeping good relations between the gods and the state.[43] They were not a "priestly caste." As such, with the exception of the flamines, they did not dedicate their lives to religious observance. They were members of the Roman aristocracy, and until the *lex Ogulnia* of 300 B.C. only patricians could be pontiffs.

The nature of the distinction between patricians and plebeians is by no means clear and is a matter of great dispute. The distinction may only have hardened in the early years of the republic. At any rate, so far back as our knowledge goes the plebeians were full citizens. The patricians can be described as the topmost aristocracy. In the strict sense of the word in the republic, the term *patres* designated only patrician senators, and their descendants were *patricii*. The senate, it should be noted, though it is always represented as the stronghold of patrician power, also included plebeian senators. Wealthy and powerful plebeian families would always be in the forefront of important political struggles between the orders.[44]

After the *lex Ogulnia*, the successful plebeian and patrician families kept the priesthoods in their own hands, keeping out outsiders. Most pontiffs were *nobiles*, that is, had ancestors who had been consuls, and many themselves held the consulship.[45] Thus, Quintus Mucius Scaevola, perhaps the most celebrated of the Republican jurists, was consul in 95 B.C., was a pontiff before that date, and became *pontifex maximus*. To him we owe important rulings on both what we would term sacred and private law.

Originally, the pontiffs were chosen by cooptation.[46] Two members of the College chose the candidates, who were limited in number to three. In the third century B.C. the *pontifex maximus* was elected from among the pontiffs by a special assembly of seventeen tribes, and a *plebiscitum* of 104 B.C. set election by the vote of seventeen tribes as the mode of appointment to all four major colleges.

One final issue should be noted. From at least the second century B.C. the Romans believed their greatness was a reward from the gods for their piety, yet it was well known that religion was manipulated—for instance, for political ends. We need not necessarily see cynicism here. What counted for the maintenance of good relations was the proper performance of the appropriate acts, and the state of mind of the participant was not relevant.

In a similar vein, without violating religious precepts, persons could "escape" the results associated with omens simply by failing to recognize them. The sign from the gods had to be recognized and accepted before it was relevant. Cicero says:

> As to divination from electrical flashes or weapons, which is entirely military, M. Marcellus, who was five times consul, commander-in-chief, and a very good augur, ignored it altogether. Indeed, he used to say that if he wished to do something he would travel in a closed litter so as not to be impeded by the auspices. Similar to this is what we augurs teach that to avoid the "auspice by the yoke" the draught-cattle be ordered unyoked. What else does a refusal to be warned by Jupiter accomplish except either to prevent an auspice from occurring or, if it occurs, to prevent it from being seen?[47]

And Pliny:

> Let these examples be enough to show that the power of omens is in our own control and that their influence depends on the way they are received. Certainly, in the teaching of the augurs it is settled that neither evil omens nor auspices affect those who at the outset of an undertaking declare that they take no notice of them. There is no greater example of divine mercy than this gift.[48]

Similarly, portents could be forced: chickens could be starved so that they would feed greedily and drop some of the grain from their beak, which was the favorable omen.[49] In such circumstances it is not surprising that prominent Romans denied belief in the force of such omens, suggesting that they (and other manifestations) were maintained for political purposes.[50] And yet there is clear evidence that powerful Romans did believe a chance word or deed could have great significance even if it were not accepted.[51]

It was said above that for good relations with the gods what mattered was the proper performance of the appropriate acts, not the state of mind of the participant. That assertion requires some qualification. Macrobius tells us in his *Saturnalia*:

> The priests declared that religious holidays were profaned if someone worked after they had been proclaimed and prescribed. Moreover, it was not permitted for the *rex sacrorum* or the flamines to see work being done during religious holidays. Thus, they had announced by means of the public crier that people had to abstain from

work and any who neglected the order were fined. [10.] In addition to the fine, it was maintained that whoever carelessly did any work on such days had to give a pig as a sin offering. The pontiff Scaevola insisted that no expiation was possible for one who acted knowingly. But Umbro said that no pollution was contracted by one who did something pertinent to the gods or on account of religion, or regarding the urgent utility of life. [11.] Then Scaevola, when he had been consulted on what it was lawful to do on holidays replied, "Anything whose omission would be harmful." Therefore, if an ox fell into a deep hole and the head of the household set him loose, with the help of his workers, he would not be seen to have profaned the holiday. Nor would one who, when the tree beam of his roof broke, preserved it by a support from imminent collapse.[52]

And Varro, *De lingua latina:*

> The contrary of these are called *dies nefasti*, "unlawful [or 'sinful'] days," on which it is *nefas*, "unlawful," for the praetor to say *do*, "I give," *dico*, "I pronounce," *addico*, "I assign." Therefore, no lawsuit can proceed. For it is necessary to use one of these words when anything is done in legal form. But if inadvertently he uttered a word and manumitted someone, that person is nonetheless free but under a bad omen, just as a magistrate elected despite a bad omen is nonetheless a magistrate. The praetor who thus spoke, if he did so inadvertently, is released from his sin by the sacrifice of a victim. If he so spoke, knowing what he was doing, Quintus Mucius said he could not atone for his impiety.[53]

Thus, if one did something that was sinful, *nefas*, the sin existed whether the act was done with or without knowledge of the wrongfulness, but the act was valid as to its consequences. But Quintus Mucius drew a distinction. If the person, such as the praetor, was inadvertent in his wrongdoing, he could expiate his sin by a sacrificial victim, but if he acted with knowledge no expiation was possible.

It has been suggested that Quintus Mucius, under the influence of Greek thought, was the originator of the distinction, making the willful violation of a religious rule beyond the power of expiation.[54] Given the important role of Mucius in legal development this possibility cannot be excluded, but it is not a necessary or even plausible inference. Mucius's legal formulation of an earlier rule may have been enough to attract subsequent attention, and the distinction is obvious and important enough to have been made early. Indeed, in a not-too-dissimilar context the distinction was being made in the third century B.C.[55] The situation is not akin to portents and prodigies. With them, no sin was involved, and their effect could properly depend on the human response, including acceptance of them. The gods need not have determined any outcome beforehand. But here the behavior is sinful, and the extent of the sin may properly depend on the violator's state of mind. But it is very revealing for Roman attitudes, and again suggestive of the minor role of the state of mind, that the sin, no matter how deliberate, does not disturb the secular legal validity of the act.[56]

We must, however, return to the issue of political manipulation of religion and of cynicism. It is notorious that there was a great deal of manipulation, cynicism, and rationalism from the latter part of the second century B.C. to the end of the republic.[57] Cicero quotes the playwright Ennius (born in 239 B.C.) on soothsayers, *haruspices:* "Soothsaying prophets and shameless gut-gazers, either clumsy or crazy, or ordered by want, who do not know their own way, point the way for another. To whom they promise riches, from them they beg a small coin. From these riches let them take the coin for themselves and hand over the rest."[58] He also quotes Pacuvius (born in 220 B.C.): "As for those who understand the language of birds and learn more wisdom from another's liver than from their own, I vote one ought to hear rather than pay attention to them."[59] Cicero also tells us that Cato the Elder (consul in 195 B.C.) said that he was amazed that one soothsayer (*haruspex*) does not laugh when he sees another.[60] Certainly, Ennius, Pacuvius, and Cato were concerned with private *haruspices,* but their words indicate a general cynicism.

As for the augurs, Accius (born in 170 B.C.) claimed, "I have no belief in augurs who enrich the ears of others with words, that they may embellish their own homes with gold."[61] It might be added that Julius Caesar was elected *pontifex maximus* in 63 B.C. after great bribery, an office that he retained until his death.[62] Pontiffs were neither a separate caste nor professional priests.[63]

The first century B.C. was an age of great rationalism for educated Romans, though it is not clear to what extent one can take the suspension of belief back to earlier days.[64] Still, it is certain that from the earliest days official Roman religion was always very much associated with the state. For instance, there was a strong tendency on the part of the leaders of the state to restrict the occasions when the populace might meet en masse,[65] and in furtherance of this, the pontiffs by the calendar restricted the days on which comitia could meet.[66] It is entirely in keeping that in the empire the jurist Ulpian could describe *ius sacrum* as part of *ius publicum*.[67]

For the very early first century B.C., we also have the revealing, though hostile, testimony of Augustine about the pontiff Scaevola, who is probably Quintus Mucius Scaevola. "It is recorded that the learned pontiff Scaevola maintained that three kinds of gods are handed down to us; one by the poets, a second by the philosophers, and a third by the leaders of the state. The first kind he says is rubbish because many unworthy tales are invented about the gods. The second, he says, is not fit for city-states, because it contains some unnecessary doctrines, and some that it is harmful for the people to know."[68] In subsequent paragraphs, Augustine discusses Scaevola's treatments of the gods as depicted by poets and philosophers. One accusation leveled against Scaevola is that he does not wish the people to know what he himself accepts as true, namely that city-states do not in fact have true images of gods, because deities have no gender or age or a well-defined bodily form. The viewpoint of Scaevola seems to be that religion, as imparted to the people, should be very much a creature of the state.

In the legal sphere, political manipulation of religion could have a powerful impact. First, elections of officials could be interfered with or the officials could be subsequently removed from office on ostensibly religious grounds. Livy gives instances from 441 B.C. onward.[69] Though the instances recorded are not numerous, we cannot tell whether there were many others, especially since books of Livy are lost. There is an obvious connection with such removals from office, as they are described, and Roman military difficulties. Second, the auspices might prevent or interrupt the meeting of an assembly.[70] Third, laws might be annulled on the basis that they were carried through by force or against the auspices. No instance of such annulment seems to be recorded before 100 B.C.[71] Such abuses were most frequent in the final years of the republic.

What is totally lacking, however, is an instance where a dispute of private law before a court was interrupted by religious manipulation.

2 The Twelve Tables: Contents

The major legal event in early Roman law was the promulgation of the Twelve Tables and this, in effect, determined the future course of legal development and the relationship of law to religion.

After the sketch of religion set out in chapter 1, stressing its centrality in Roman public life, the Twelve Tables present us with a surprise. Religion seems totally absent. The Twelve Tables contain nothing about state cults, functions, or acts of priests, and nothing about the preservation of private cults. Moreover, substantive private law, as it seems to have been at the time, whether set out in the code or not, also almost entirely lacked a sacred character. No religious ceremony, prayer, or invocation of the gods was required for the transfer of property, even of land, and no oath was involved in making a contract. Of the three forms creating marriage with *manus* (that is, a marriage in which the wife came into the power of the head of her husband's family), only one, *confarreatio* (and its related form of divorce, *diffarreatio*), required priestly involvement for its legal efficacy.[1] Of the parts of the law that we would regard as private law that did need priestly involvement—namely, marriage by *confarreatio*, adoption of the type called *adrogatio*, and the making of a will *calatis comitiis* (that is, in the assembly)—only the first was, I believe, mentioned in the codification and, at that, only incidentally.[2] Surprisingly, also, given the significance of verbal formulations for Roman religion, we find no indication that the Twelve Tables contained any forms for performing an act in the law: not for bringing an action, not for the contract of *stipulatio*, not for the transfer of ownership by *mancipatio*, not for marriage by *confarreatio*.

To estimate the significance of this we must establish the nature of the Twelve Tables. And before this can be done, the survival rate of the provisions must be uncovered, and any bias in the proportion of survivals determined. These are two separate issues. If only a small proportion of the provisions has survived, it may not be significant if whole areas of the law have disappeared from our sight. If there is a bias in the survival rate, then even if a substantial proportion of the provisions has survived, whole areas of the law may still have disappeared.

This second issue will be treated in due course, but it should be stated at the outset that, as will emerge, by no means all legal institutions existing at the time of the Twelve Tables were dealt with in the code. For a provision to be inserted there had to be a particular reason, such as a change in the law. Absence of sacred law from the Twelve Tables is, therefore, not in itself inconsistent with its presence in the law. Any absence, though, will have to be accounted for.

Unlike modern codes, the Twelve Tables did not aim at completeness, and major subjects of private law that existed at that time were omitted.[3] Most of these can be established thanks to Quintus Mucius Scaevola's (consul 95 B.C., *pontifex maximus*) work, *Ius Civile*. The commentary can be reconstructed in large measure,[4] and it emerges in the first place that Mucius's conception of civil law was statute law. No topic that was not dealt with by statute or that could not be brought by attraction within the scope of a statutory provision was dealt with.[5] Therefore, a topic of private law existing as early as the Twelve Tables that is not evidenced elsewhere as being dealt with in the code and that is not treated in Quintus Mucius's *Ius Civile* probably was not dealt with in the code, or at least the provision had not reached Quintus Mucius. That most provisions would have survived to his time will be shown shortly.

Matters of private law omitted from the Twelve Tables can be listed as follows:

1. The requirements for marriage, including minimum age, necessary consents, prohibited degrees of relationship and personal status. But one provision was included, that prohibiting intermarriage between patrician and plebeian.[6] This is always presented in the sources as an innovation: so it must have been, and that is why the rule was inserted.[7]

2. Dowry. This was not included because there were no rules specifically on dowry, though it could be created by promising it by *stipulatio*, or by delivering it.[8]

3. *Stipulatio*, the oldest Roman contract, whether with regard to its form or its effects. Presumably the law on *stipulatio* was regarded as settled, since the contract of *depositum*, which is perhaps more recent, was the subject of a clause.[9]

4. Slavery, including the grounds for enslavement and manumission.[10] There was, however, a provision on the *statuliber* (that is, a slave who by a will was to be freed when a condition was fulfilled).[11]

5. The *testamentum comitiis calatis* (the will made in the *comitia calata*). In contrast, the *testamentum per aes et libram* (will by bronze and scales) was dealt with, presumably because it arose in practice without official authorization as an adaptation of *mancipatio*, and the code was confirming its validity.[12]

6. The ways of acquiring (but not of transferring) ownership, with the exception of *usus* (long use). These are: *occupatio* (the taking of what was not already owned), *fructuum separatio,* or *perceptio* (the separation or gathering of fruits), *thesauri inventio* (the finding of treasure), *accessio* (the joining of things belonging to different owners), and *specificatio* (the making of a new thing out of things belonging to different owners).[13]

The treatment of *usus* in the code provides strong evidence of the validity of the approach taken in this part of the chapter. We have evidence of no fewer than six rules on prescription of property, and together they give a comprehensive account of the topic.[14] It is hard to imagine that mere chance would dictate both the survival of so much material on *usus* and also the destruction of much on other ways of acquiring ownership. Rather, we should believe that there was a specific reason for dealing with *usus* but not with the others—namely, that *usus* was an innovation.[15]

7. The three basic issues for theft (which the Romans treated primarily as a private wrong, the delict of *furtum*), namely, (*a*) the physical activity needed to commit theft; (*b*) the necessary state of mind in the wrongdoer; and (*c*) the basis of the distinction between *furtum manifestum* and *furtum nec manifestum*.[16] This time we have exact proof that the last was not contained in a provision in the code, since the basis for the distinction between "manifest" and "nonmanifest" was still being debated in the time of Justinian, a millennium later, with never a mention of the Twelve Tables. Yet there was a number of provisions on lesser aspects of theft.[17]

It is important to establish that such major topics of private law were not treated in the Twelve Tables, because otherwise we would exaggerate the extent of their loss. Though statistics cannot be produced, it would seem—once omissions are taken into account—that we have knowledge of a high proportion of the Twelve Tables' provisions on private law.[18]

But to estimate the treatment of sacred law in the code we still have to consider the second issue, namely survival bias. Our sources of knowledge of the Twelve Tables are texts from much later writers who describe the impact of particular provisions or who purport to give the exact wording—though much modernized—and an interpretation. Not all writers were interested in all topics equally. If, for instance, all our information came only from legal sources, we would expect a marked bias toward private law. There is, after all, little sacred law, especially antique sacred law, in Gaius's *Institutes* and in the *Corpus Juris Civilis*, and not a great deal of public law. If we had to rely on these works for our information on the Twelve Tables, then we could deduce little about the role of the sacred in the code. In fact, less than fifty percent of our knowledge comes from them.

Much, therefore, depends on the nature of our other sources of information. This knowledge comes from a number of writers, such as Cicero, Varro, Festus, Aulus Gellius, and Pliny the Elder.

One might expect a survival bias against sacred law provisions in most of Cicero's speeches. But the contrary would be true of some other speeches, such as *De domo* and *Pro haruspicum responso*, which involve religious issues. Most of his oratorical and philosophical writings would be unlikely to show a survival bias in favor of either private or sacred law. But some at least, notably *De divinatione* and *De legibus* (which latter deals in its surviving parts largely with religious law), would be more likely to produce evidence on sacred than on private law provisions of the code, and they provide none.

An important source of information on the Twelve Tables is the *De lingua latina* of M. Terentius Varro (116–27 B.C.), of which only books 5 to 10 (partly) survive. These books concern the etymology and the formation of Latin words, and such a grammatical work ought to show no survival bias. In fact, it contains much information on Roman religion, though none on sacred law in the Twelve Tables. Also important are the surviving books 12 to 20 of Sextus Pompeius Festus's abridgement of Verrius Flaccus's *De verborum significatu* in the second century A.D. In this work, too, there could be no marked bias for or against the survival rate of religious-law provisions in the Twelve Tables. Likewise without any marked survival bias should be the *Noctes Atticae* of Aulus Gellius, of the second century A.D., who discusses various issues of philosophy, textual criticism, legal science, and religion.[19] The same should be true of the massive *Historia naturalis* of C. Plinius Secundus (23/24–79 A.D.) and of the writings of literary commentators such as Servius (on Virgil). In Macrobius's *Saturnalia*, of the fifth century, the bias should even be toward the survival of sacred-law provisions, since he deals with the Saturnalian festivals, the Roman calendar, and the Neoplatonic synthesis of the deities in book 1 (augural science in lost books 2 and part of 3) and pontifical law in surviving parts of book 3.

Thus, we cannot attribute our total absence of knowledge of provisions concerning official, and private cult, religion in the Twelve Tables to any lack of interest on the part of writers of such surviving works as are of importance for understanding private law in the Twelve Tables.

Nor can it plausibly be maintained that knowledge of any such provisions was lost prior to Cicero and the others. About 200 B.C. Sextus Aelius Paetus

Catus wrote his *Tripertita* (The three parts), which preserved knowledge of the Twelve Tables for subsequent Romans.[20] Its three parts were, first, each clause of the Twelve Tables, then its interpretation, and lastly the relevant action in the law. Not much that was recorded by Sextus Aelius would be lost to later Romans. Cicero, indeed, records that in his youth children learned the Twelve Tables by heart, presumably from this version.[21] But what was lost for Sextus Aelius would remain lost. Still, for a number of reasons, this cannot explain any suggested loss of sacred-law provisions. To begin with, the interest in religion in Sextus Aelius's time was intense. Second, much of the old religious rules survived, hence there would be practical interest in any such provisions in the code, so they would not disappear from view. Third, in any event, Sextus Aelius discusses provisions of private law that were obsolete in his time and even not understood.[22] If knowledge of such had survived, then equally so would knowledge of even obsolete provisions of sacred law. Fourth, and this is the clincher, before the Twelve Tables, the second king, Numa Pompilius, is recorded as having issued much legislation on sacred law, and considerable information on such has survived. Indeed, we even have sources purporting to give the actual wording of the provisions. Knowledge of these laws and their contexts comes from numerous different sources: Livy, Cicero, Pliny the Elder, Aulus Gellius, Festus, Servius, Lydus, Dionysius of Halicarnassus, and Plutarch.[23] In such circumstances, it is inconceivable that, if the Twelve Tables had contained provisions on sacred law, all information on them would have been lost.

What has to be emphasized is the pattern. It is not that we have evidence of fewer provisions than we might have expected on state cults, priestly functions, preservation of private cults, religious elements in private law, and the necessary forms for acts in the law. We have no evidence of any such provisions. And we must conclude such provisions never existed.

The one apparent exception to the above provides confirmation. The jurist Gaius records: "for the early lawyers wanted women, even if they were of full age, to be in guardianship because of their instability of judgment . . . except for the Vestal Virgins whom even the ancients wished to be free from authority in honor of their priestly office: and this was even laid down in the Twelve Tables."[24] Thus, the only surviving provision that mentions the holder of a priestly office regulates an issue of private law!

But we must ask, even tentatively at this stage, why there were no such provisions. The state religion and priestly functions were at that date preserves of the patricians, and therefore no fit subject for legislation that was ostensibly made under duress from the plebeians. This is discussed further in chapter 3. For the absence of forms two explanations are equally plausible. One possibility is based on the fact that the legislation was never comprehensive. It may be suggested that the forms were omitted because they were settled, and no innovation was being made in them.

The other possibility is that the Twelve Tables were not a success for the plebeians who, according to Livy, wanted to know what the law was.[25] The codification gave them the rules, but not the forms needed to bring the rules into play: how to formulate an action, transfer property (which was *res mancipi*), or make a contract. Still, according to Livy, C. Terentilius Harsa, tribune of the plebs, expressly wanted the codification to define and limit the powers of the consuls. This the plebeians did not get. The significance of this will also be further discussed in chapter 3.

A different explanation must be given for the absence of traces of religious elements from the provisions of the Twelve Tables on private law, and from most of private law in general. The explanation is that in general there were no religious elements in Roman private law. From very early times, Roman private law, in our modern sense of the term, was very much a secular subject.[26] The significance of this will emerge later when we have examined the points where religion and law do interact.

On the view that we have some knowledge of most of the provisions of the Twelve Tables, it is appropriate to list what these covered. Most prominent is private law, followed by procedure. Some aspects of what we should regard as criminal law are treated; there are sumptuary and hygienic rules on the disposal of the dead; and there is one hygienic rule to kill quickly a deformed baby.[27] Public law, in the sense of the appointment, powers, and duties of public officials, is entirely absent.

Given the subject matter of this book it is appropriate to observe that some crimes punish the use of magic—not necessarily the same thing as religion—by the wrongdoer, and that some crimes have a religious element, especially in the punishment.

Thus, to weave a magic spell was punishable by death;[28] it was an offense to enchant away another's crops or decoy another's corn into one's own field.[29] On the other hand, for pasturing or cutting secretly another's crops that had been acquired by tillage, a person above puberty was to be hanged as a sacrifice to Ceres;[30] and a patron who defrauded a client was to be *sacer*.[31] If a weapon fled from a person's hand rather than having been thrown, a ram was substituted as a sacrifice.[32] The Twelve Tables also forbade, with a double penalty, consecrating anything as sacred about which there was a legal dispute.[33] The very limited nature of these provisions tells its own story.[34] Finally, a form of action that involved an oath was provided. This *legis actio sacramento* is discussed in chapter 4.

To end on a different note, the Twelve Tables are very much "pure law," and in this they stand in contrast to some other bodies of law, such as the Ten Commandments. Totally missing from the Roman codification is anything resembling "Honor your father and your mother, that you may live long in the land which the Lord your God is giving you."[35] That prescription is a general principle that either gives no law or only very indirectly can be turned into a rule with legal content. The reason expressed for the prescription is not a legal one, and there is no legal sanction.[36] This "lawness" of the Twelve Tables is also to be found earlier at Rome, in the supposed laws of the kings. They are discussed in chapter 12.

3 The Twelve Tables: The Public/Private Law Distinction

The Twelve Tables, as we have seen in the preceding chapter, omitted altogether public law and sacred law. We have here, apparently, the beginnings of the famous distinction between public and private law that has been so prominent and important in subsequent Western law.

The systematic distinction between public and private law does not appear in earlier civilizations and it will not have existed before at Rome.[1] Though sacred law was possibly already separate and the pontiffs determined what was and was not permitted without causing an injury in the religious sphere, the pontiffs, as we have seen, also were and long remained the guardians of official pronouncements on what we must consider as private law.

Further, the distinction between sacred, public, and private law also cannot have been intended to be made in the Twelve Tables. To begin with, the distinction between public and private law is expressly made only much later.[2] Second, the Twelve Tables certainly cannot be said to be only a compilation of private substantive law: they also contain procedure, criminal law, sumptuary legislation (relating to disposal of the dead), and hygienic regulations. Third, we have no indication of any theory of classification for the codification. Last, in any event, such classification would be an unparalleled theoretical feat for early Roman law. A glance at the arrangement of the praetor's Edict or of Quintus Mucius's commentary on the *ius civile* would show how little interested the Romans were in the organization of legal categories even in the late republic.[3]

To explain the omission of public and sacred law we should look at the history of the making of the Twelve Tables. We have two main accounts, that of Livy and that of Dionysius of Halicarnassus.[4]

Livy's version is entirely self-consistent. In the years before the codification (and later) there was great tension and hostility between the patricians and plebeians, and the plebeians' political demands centered on the need for law reform.[5] Livy describes the events of 462 B.C.

Thus, affairs at Rome returned to their old condition, and success in war at once led to disturbances in the city. [2.] C. Terentilius Harsa was that year a tribune of the plebs. He considered that the absence of the consul gave the opportunity for tribunician activity, and on several days he inveighed against patrician arrogance to the plebs, and especially against the powers of the consuls, which he said were excessive and intolerable in a free state. [3.] Only in name was the word "consul" less hateful than "king": the fact of consular government was almost more horrible than a monarchy. [4.] For they had accepted two masters instead of one, with unlimited and infinite power, who, free from all restraint and with no check upon themselves, turned all fear of the laws and all punishments against the plebs. [5.] So that they should not have such license for ever, he would propose a law that five men be appointed to the task of writing down the laws on the powers of the consuls. The consuls would use the law given them by the people, and they would not treat their own unrestrained passion as if it were statute.[6]

Thus, for Livy, the first demand of the plebs was precisely what they did not get in the Twelve Tables or in any similar legislation: laws setting out and restricting the powers of the consuls. No progress, he then says, was made that year, but in the following year Terentilius again brought his proposal forward with the backing of all the tribunes, only to be faced by numerous omens, including a rain of lumps of meat.[7] The Sybilline books were inspected by the relevant two officials who found danger of external attack and, significantly, a warning against factious politics. The tribunes of the plebs declared this to be a fraudulent attempt to prevent the passing of the law. Insistence on the law continued on the part of the tribunes and still remained the main concern.[8] At one stage, in 460 B.C., the consul Cincinnatus was driven to say to the people, "Sunk as you are in crimes against the gods and men, you still maintain you will pass the law this year."[9] So the plebeian demand was regarded as against religion as well as against political order.

About 454 B.C. the consuls declared that the one thing that would not happen was the passage of a law by the people and the tribunes.[10] This time the tribunes were discouraged and they proposed a compromise. If the senate would not accept a law passed by the people, then the tribunes suggested that both sides might appoint a team of lawmakers from the plebeians and the patricians to make laws beneficial to both sides and to equalize the liberty of both. The senators were not against the idea in principle but insisted that only they could make law. This was accepted by the plebs, and a team was sent to Athens (it is reported) to write down the famous laws of Solon and to discover the laws and customs of other Greek states.[11]

There was tranquility at Rome while the delegation was away,[12] but then Livy records:

> The next consuls were C. Menenius and P. Sestius Capitolinus. Nor was there any external war that year, though there was disturbance at home. [6.] The legation had come back with the Attic laws. The tribunes insisted all the more that at last a beginning be made to writing the law. It was decided to appoint ten men [*decemviri*] from whom there could be no appeal, and that in that year there would be no other public official. [7.] There was some controversy as to whether plebeians could be appointed, but in the end the plebeians gave way to the patricians, on the understanding that the *lex Icilia* about the Aventine and the other sacred laws would not be abrogated.[13]

The *lex Icilia*, about which the plebs were so concerned, was a plebiscite the senate had had to ratify, which granted the Aventine hill to the poorest citizens for settlement.[14]

Dionysius of Halicarnassus's account is to much the same effect as Livy's.[15] He says, for the year 459 B.C.:

> The year after their consulship occurred the eightieth Olympiad (the one at which Torymbas, a Thessalian, won the foot-race), Phrasicles being archon at Athens; and Publius Volumnius and Servius Sulpicius Camerinus were chosen consuls at Rome. These men led no army into the field, either to take revenge on those who had injured the Romans themselves as well as their allies or to keep guard over their possessions, but they devoted their attention to the domestic evils, fearing lest the populace might organize against the senate and work some mischief. [2.] For they were being stirred up again by the tribunes and instructed that the best of political institutions for free men is an equality of rights; and they demanded that all business both private and public should be carried on according to laws. For at that time there did not exist as yet among the Romans an equality either of laws or of rights, nor were all their principles of justice committed to writing; but at first their kings had dispensed justice to those who sought it, and whatever they decreed was law. [3.] After they ceased to be governed by kings, along with the other functions of royalty that of determining what justice is devolved upon the annual consuls, and it was they who decided what was just between litigants in any matter whatsoever. [4.] These decisions as a rule conformed to the character of the magistrates, who were appointed to office on the basis of good birth. A very few of the decisions, however, were kept in sacred books and had the force of laws; but the patricians alone were acquainted with these, because they spent their time in the capital, while the masses, who were either merchants or husbandmen and came down to the capital only for the markets at intervals of many days, were as yet unfamiliar with them. [5.] The

first attempt to introduce this measure establishing an equality of rights was made by Gaius Terentius in the preceding year, while he was tribune; but he was forced to leave the business unfinished because the plebeians were then in the field and the consuls purposely detained the armies in the enemy's country till their term of office expired.[16]

To prevent the legislation, the consuls, senators, and other leading people resorted to all manner of tricks;[17] there occurred the portents described by Livy, and the Sybilline books were also read to the same effect. Both sides claimed the other was the one responsible for civil strife:

> These and many like reproaches were uttered by each side for many days and the time passed in vain; meanwhile no business in the city, either public or private, was being brought to completion. When nothing worthwhile was being accomplished, the tribunes desisted from the kind of harangues and accusations they were wont to make against the senate; and calling an assembly of the populace, they promised them to bring in a law embodying their demands. [4.] This being approved of by the populace, they read without further delay the law which they had prepared, the chief provisions of which were as follows: That ten men should be chosen by the people meeting in a legitimate assembly, men who were at once the oldest and the most prudent and had the greatest regard for honor and a good reputation; that these men should draw up the laws concerning all matters both public and private and lay them before the people; and that the laws to be drawn up by them should be exposed in the forum for the benefit of the magistrates who should be chosen each year and also of persons in private station, as a code defining the mutual rights of citizens.[18]

The measure proposed by the tribunes was, it will be noticed, for the enactment of statutes covering both public and private law.

The response of the consuls and patricians was to maintain that the tribunes and the plebs had not the right to make or abrogate laws, and that they, the patricians, would not permit them to do so. They also pointed out that, on the election of tribunes, sacrifices were not made in accordance with law nor was anything observed in their office that was holy.[19] The struggle continued. Events are substantially recorded as in Livy, but Dionysius states expressly that it was Romilius of the patrician side who suggested the embassy to Greek cities. Romilius declared:

> "The substance of my advice is that you choose ambassadors and send some of them to the Greek cities in Italy and others to Athens, to ask the Greeks for their best laws and such as are most suited to our ways of life, and then to bring these laws here. And when they return, that the consuls then in office shall propose for the consider-

ation of the senate what men to choose as lawgivers, what magistracy they shall hold and for how long a time, and to determine everything else in such a manner as they shall think expedient; and that you contend no longer with the plebeians nor add calamities to your calamities, particularly by quarreling over laws which, if nothing else, have at least a respectable reputation for dignity." [20]

Eventually, on the return of the ambassadors, the senate decreed the preparation of a body of law by *decemviri*, a decree accepted with enthusiasm by the tribunes.[21]

Thus goes the story of the background to the Twelve Tables, as told by the sources. If we may take it as a substantially accurate account of the tensions and struggles, then the Twelve Tables do not mark a complete victory for the plebeians. They wanted to make the law. They lost that point completely according to the fuller account of Dionysius. It was the senate that passed the decree establishing the *decemviri*.[22] And the *decemviri* had to be, and were, all patricians, according to both Dionysius and Livy.[23] And the laws enacting the Twelve Tables were the work of the *comitia centuriata* which was controlled by the patricians.[24] According to Livy, what the plebeians wanted in their demand for law reform was a law—actually they wanted a *plebiscitum*—setting out and restricting the powers of the consuls. According to Dionysius, the plebeians wanted equality of law, and enactments on both public and private law. They got none of this.

Against this background, it is not at all surprising that the Twelve Tables contain only those matters that the patricians would consider fit subjects for the attention of the plebs. Official or state religious law is omitted. First, religion is the business of the main colleges of priests, all of whom are patricians. Second, that religion is concerned above all with maintaining the right balance between the gods and the state, with the proper religious formalities involving magistrates and assemblies. Third, the Roman official religion is not much concerned with the religious behavior of ordinary individuals. That is why already, as we shall see, Roman private law is so secular in appearance.[25] Roman public law, in the sense of the election and duties of consuls and other magistrates and the functioning of the senate and the comitia, is excluded precisely because the patricians did not want these to be the concern of the plebeians. Law relating to the tribunes of the plebs or the *concilium plebis* is omitted either because that did not interest the patrician *decemviri* as being purely plebeian matters or more plausibly because it was politically unwise for the patricians to seem to be tinkering with plebeian rights.

This explanation illuminates the two provisions of the Twelve Tables that alone might be said to concern public law,[26] though not in the sense defined above. These apparently ran somewhat as follows: "Tab. 9.1. No law of personal exception shall be proposed." That is, no law is to be passed punishing an individual who has not broken a general rule of the community. "Tab. 9.2. No procedure is to be brought against the life of a citizen or against his citizenship except before the greatest assembly [i.e., presumably the *comitia centuriata*]."[27] These are best seen as concessions. The plebs, as is constantly emphasized, wanted equality of legal treatment, and they wanted the arbitrary behavior of consuls restrained. These ameliorations they did not get, but they did win these valuable rights of civil liberties. The concessions should be compared with that obtained when the tribunes agreed that the *decemviri* would all be patricians, namely that the *lex Icilia* would not be abrogated.

Thus, the first de facto separation of public law from private law was not intended to mark a theoretical division of two contrasting areas of law, but resulted from particular historical events.[28] Sacred law had perhaps to some extent separated even earlier, but the separation here was reinforced by the same historical events. The nature of Roman official religion had itself ensured that the rules of substantive private law would be overtly secular.

The prominence of the Twelve Tables made it certain that the separation of private from public law would have a considerable impact. But the division was to be given increased effect by another historical event. Pomponius, the only Roman jurist who to our knowledge wrote expressly on the history of law, relates:

When these laws [i.e., specifically the Twelve Tables] were enacted (as it naturally happens that interpretation requires the authority of experts) forensic debate became necessary. This debate and this law which was formed without formal writing by experts is not called by a particular name as other parts of law are denoted by their own names (their own names being given to other parts), but is called by the common name, civil law [*ius civile*]. [6.] Then, almost at the same time, actions were formed from these laws, which men could use in their disputes. Lest people would frame actions as they wished, the lawmakers wanted them to be fixed and formal, and this part of the law is called "actions of the law" [*legis actiones*], that is, statutory actions. And so, almost at the same time, these three branches of law were born. The Twelve Tables were passed, from them began to flow the civil law, from them, too, the actions of the law were formed. The science of interpreting all these and the actions were in the hands of the College of Pontiffs, from among whom one was appointed each year for interpreting private-law matters.[29]

Since the College of Pontiffs had long been in the business of interpreting sacred law and were also the guardians, before the codification, of general legal regulations which had no specifically sacred character, it was natural that they be entrusted with the task of interpreting the Twelve Tables. But the pontiffs each year allotted this task to one of their number, in this way keeping jurisdiction over private-law matters separate from the general jurisdiction of all the pontiffs in sacred law. The task allotted to this one individual was, we are told by Pomponius, specifically that of interpreting the Twelve Tables, not legislation in general.[30] And from this interpretation developed civil law. In this sense, and it is not the only one, *ius civile* was the received scholarly interpretation of the Twelve Tables. And this interpretation would have to take account of statutes derogating from the Twelve Tables.

It is this conception of *ius civile* that first begins to let us understand fully the nature of Quintus Mucius Scaevola's commentary of the same name. He restricts the notion of *ius civile* to the interpretation of the Twelve Tables and of statutes that altered it. That is why topics such as slave law and the law of dowry, which are certainly part of the "civil law" in the wider understanding of that term, are not discussed by him. They were not treated in the code, hence any legal rules that emerged were not interpretation of the Twelve Tables and thus not relevant for inclusion in Mucius's *Ius Civile*. Likewise, legislation subsequent to the Twelve Tables but not derogating from it, that is, especially on public law, would not count as *ius civile*.

This last point requires expansion. The latest statute for private law dealt with by Quintus Mucius which we know about is the *lex Aquilia* of about 287 B.C., a fact that gives his work the surprising appearance of being very much out of date.[31] The explanation is that Quintus Mucius was writing a commentary on the interpretation of the Twelve Tables, and these subsequent private-law enactments later than the Twelve Tables either did not deal with topics included in that code or were obsolete before the time of Justinian (and hence Mucius's treatment has been lost, since the topics do not appear in Justinian's codification). In contrast the *lex Aquilia* modified the Twelve Tables.[32] Thus, the *lex Appuleia de sponsu* (sometime after 241 B.C.), the *lex Furia* (perhaps of about 200 B.C.), and the *lex Cincia* (whose date cannot be established) all concerned personal guarantees which were made by using the *stipulatio*, which was not dealt with in the Twelve Tables. The *lex Cincia* (of 204 B.C.) above all forbade gifts above a certain amount, and the *lex Plaetoria* (slightly later) dealt with fraud on a minor: neither gifts nor minors were treated in the archaic code. The *lex Minicia* (before 90 B.C.) said that children born to parents who did not have the capacity for civil-law marriage took the lower status. Neither the requirements for marriage (apart from the prohibition of intermarriage between plebeian and patrician) nor status was dealt with in the Twelve Tables. The *lex Atilia* (of, perhaps, 210 B.C.) and the *lex Titia* (of about 99 B.C.) concerned the appointment of tutors by public officials to persons who had none. *Tutela* was, in fact, extensively treated in the Twelve Tables,[33] and we might have expected Mucius to have dealt with these two statutes. But if he did, as he might well have done, his treatment would have left no trace in the *Digest*. These particular statutes, *lex Atilia* and *lex Titia*, fell out of use in the early empire,[34] and (although they are mentioned in Justinian's *Institutes*) they do not at all appear in the *Digest* where alone we find references to Quintus Mucius and his *Ius Civile*. Moreover, for some unclear reason, no text dealing with *tutela* (even in the Twelve Tables) has survived from Pomponius's commentary on Quintus Mucius. This leaves unaccounted for in Quintus Mucius only the *lex Furia testamentaria* (somewhere between 204 and 169 B.C.) and the *lex Voconia* (of 169 B.C.), both of which concern testamentary succession which was dealt with in the Twelve Tables. Both of these statutes are referred to in numerous texts, but the significant point for us is that, as with the *lex Atilia* and the *lex Titia*, their rules did not survive until the time of Justinian and in fact neither statute is referred to in any part of the *Corpus Juris Civilis*.[35] Thus, Quintus Mucius may very well have dealt with these statutes, and Pomponius in his commentary on Mucius may also have discussed them, but no trace would have been left.

On this view, we can now understand why we have no sign of discussion in Quintus Mucius's *Ius Civile* of any statute later than the *lex Aquilia*. His topic was the interpretation of the Twelve Tables.

For this narrow conception of *ius civile*, which was by no means necessary,[36] it is probably relevant that Quintus Mucius was long a pontiff and was even *pontifex maximus*.[37] The College of Pontiffs had long since lost its monopoly of interpretation, but the pontiffs remained interested, and the tradition of their function would remain alive in the college. The authoritative interpretation of law that was granted to the College of Pontiffs was specifically that of the Twelve Tables.

We cannot tell from Quintus Mucius's *Ius Civile* whether he had narrowed its notion of interpretation of the Twelve Tables and restricted his commentary to what we would term private law, excluding consideration of criminal law, of the two clauses on civil liberties, and of procedure. The problem is that these topics might easily have been discussed near the end of the commentary, and we have no indication of the contents of the last two of Quintus Mucius's eighteen books of *Ius Civile*, since no texts from them have survived.[38]

Certainly by the time of Cicero the distinction between *ius privatum* and *ius publicum* was being clearly made.[39] This seems remarkably early and in its turn is best considered to be a consequence of the contents of the Twelve Tables.

One final point is appropriate in this chapter. In early Rome, before the Twelve Tables, the primary division in law was into human law (*ius*) and divine law (*fas*). For the jurist Ulpian the main division was other: "Of this discipline there are two branches, public and private. Public law is that which relates to the circumstances of the Roman commonwealth, private which relates to the interest of individuals. Public law covers sacred acts, priests, and state officers. Private law is in three parts: for it is brought together from principles of natural law, law of nations, and the law of the state."[40] The question—to which an answer will subsequently be given—is, Why is law divided into two branches? and why these two branches? Elsewhere, where he is less concerned with divisions, Ulpian has: "Justice is the steady and enduring intention to give everyone his right. [1.] The precepts of the law are these: to live honestly; not to injure another; to give to each his right. [2.] The science of law is the knowledge of things divine and human, the awareness of justice and injustice."[41] For Ulpian, the science of law entails knowledge of things divine and human, but the primary division of law is into public and private law. Public law includes sacred law. Roman official religion is very much part of the state, a function of the government.

4 Formalism in Religion and Law

Tarquinius Superbus, the seventh king of Rome, wished to fulfill his grandfather's vow to erect temples to Jupiter, Juno, and Minerva. While the foundations were being dug, a prodigy appeared. At a great depth in the ground a freshly killed human head was discovered. It appeared like that of a living man, and the blood that flowed from it was warm and fresh. Tarquinius ordered work to cease and summoned the soothsayers, who admitted they could not interpret the prodigy and that the Etruscans were the real experts. Tarquinius sent ambassadors to the most distinguished Etruscan expert.[1] Then:

> When these men came to the house of the soothsayer they met by chance a youth who was just coming out, and informing him that they were ambassadors sent from Rome who wanted to speak with the soothsayer, they asked him to announce them to him. The youth replied: "The man you wish to speak with is my father. He is busy at present, but in a short time you may be admitted to him. And while you are waiting for him, acquaint me with the reason for your coming. [2.] For if, through inexperience, you are in danger of committing an error in phrasing your question, when you have been informed by me you will be able to avoid any mistake; for the correct form of question is not the least important part of the art of divination."
> The ambassadors resolved to follow his advice and related the prodigy to him. And when the youth had heard it, after a short pause he said: "Hear me, Romans. My father will interpret this prodigy to you and will tell you no untruth, since it is not right for a soothsayer to speak falsely; but, in order that you may be guilty of no error or falsehood in what you say or in the answers you give to his questions (for it is of importance to you to know these things beforehand), be instructed by me. [3.] After you have related the prodigy to him he will tell you that he does not fully understand what you say and will circumscribe with his staff some piece of ground or other; then he will say to you: 'This is the Tarpeian Hill, and this is the part of it that faces the east, this the part that faces the west, this point is north and the opposite is south.' [4.] These parts he will point out to you with his staff and then ask you in which of these parts the head was found. What answer, therefore, do I advise you

to make? Do not admit that the prodigy was found in any of these places he shall inquire about when he points them out with his staff, but say that it appeared among you at Rome on the Tarpeian Hill. If you stick to these answers and do not allow yourselves to be misled by him, he, well knowing that fate cannot be changed, will interpret to you without concealment what the prodigy means."

[61.1.] Having received these instructions, the ambassadors, as soon as the old man was at leisure and a servant came out to fetch them, went in and related the prodigy to the soothsayer. He, craftily endeavoring to mislead them, drew circular lines upon the ground and then other straight lines, and asked them with reference to each place in turn whether the head had been found there; but the ambassadors, not at all disturbed in mind, stuck to the one answer suggested to them by the soothsayer's son, always naming Rome and the Tarpeian Hill, and asked the interpreter not to appropriate the omen to himself, but to answer in the most sincere and just manner. [2.] The soothsayer, accordingly, finding it impossible for him either to impose upon the men or to appropriate the omen, said to them: "Romans, tell your fellow citizens it is ordained by fate that the place in which you found the head shall be the head of all Italy." Since that time the place is called the Capitoline Hill from the head that was found there; for the Romans call heads *capita*.[2]

Thus, the prodigy existed; its meaning was fixed, but the effect of that meaning depended on the precise conduct, especially the verbal formulation, of the Romans when the prodigy was first being explained. The soothsayer may not lie, but he is properly entitled to deceive.[3] And successful deception will have a powerful impact on the effect of the prodigy. The same religious right to deceive but with no right to misstate or power to change the meaning of a prodigy adheres to the Roman augurs and other priests. This is likewise the case with future portents. There may be deliberate manipulation to effect the outcome—the sacred chickens may be starved so that grain falls from their greedy beaks—with an effect produced in the portent which nonetheless retains its meaning. But the priests cannot misstate what occurred with any impact on the future. No cynicism is necessarily involved in this approach, but the religion has little to do with ideas of morality. The outward form of the human acts or the verbal formulation is what produces the effect. It will be observed that manipulation was inherent in Roman religion from the start.

With prayer and sacrifices, too, extreme attention was paid to the proper words spoken and to the proper acts:[4]

> In fact, the sacrifice of victims without the prayer is said to be of no effect. The gods have not been properly consulted. [11.] Moreover, there are different sets of words for obtaining one's demands, for averting harm, for a commendation. We see that

our chief magistrates have adopted fixed formulations of prayer and lest any word be left out or be out of place, a reader first dictates, another is appointed a guardian to keep watch, and another is appointed to keep a strict silence, a flute player plays so that nothing but the prayer is heard.[5]

A mistake in the wording or act meant that the prayer or ceremony was ineffective and had to be repeated.[6] Indeed, where the mistake in the ceremony occurred during the ceremonial games, the games had to be repeated: "If the dancer stood still, or the flute player suddenly was silent, or if the boy whose two parents were living did not keep to the chariot or let the reins drop, or if the aedile erred in the wording or in handling the sacred vessel, the games were not duly performed, expiation has to be made for the mistakes, and the feelings of the immortal gods are appeased by the games being begun again."[7] According to Cassius Dio, *Roman History*, 60.6.4, a mistake might require the games to be repeated up to ten times. Plutarch, *Coriolanus* 25.3, who, we may assume, exaggerates, says that a sacrifice might be repeated thirty times because an error was thought to occur.[8] What was truly dangerous in the performance of the religious rites was not the error that was noticed—that could be rectified—but the error that was not caught. Hence the elaborate precautions.

In law, in contrast, relatively few institutions required formalities, whether of wording or of act, for legal effectiveness.[9] Formalities were not required for the creation of marriage or of most contracts, or for the transfer of property classed as *res nec mancipi*. The main institutions involving formalities were *stipulatio* in contract, *mancipatio* in property law, and the old *legis actiones* in procedure.

The basic form and formalities of the *stipulatio* were very simple in classical law. The promisor asked the promisee if he would promise to give or do something, and the promisee promised without any lapse of time and without qualification, necessarily using the same verb.[10] In early times only one verb could appropriately be used, *spondere*, and this retained the characteristic that later, when the verbs could be used, it created a legal obligation between Roman citizens alone, and was not legally effective when used by peregrines.[11]

The *stipulatio*, especially for the time when only *spondere* could be used, is a fine parallel to formal words in Roman religious observance. The speaking of the required words creates the bond and serves notice on the parties that they are engaged in something serious, in this case making a contract. It does not fulfill the other usual functions of formalities that we find in contract in other legal systems but that do not exist in religion, namely, to provide evidence for a court or other outsiders in the event of a dispute of the existence of the contract or of the terms of the contract.[12] It thus is all the more striking that originally *stipulatio* was the sole Roman contract.

The *stipulatio* is probably to be linked directly to proto-Roman religion. The same concept of the power of the appropriate verbal formulation imbues both the Roman prayer and sacrifice on the one hand, and the *stipulatio* on the other. This would seem to be confirmed by the fact that the etymological root of the word *spondere* is the Greek σπονδή, "a libation." The obligation arose from the ritual.[13]

It is in line with such an origin linked with Roman religion that the promisor is bound strictly by the actual verbal terms of his promise. The words will be enforced, and surrounding circumstances will not be relevant. A careless framing of the wording in the promise, error as to what or why he is promising, or fraud or coercion by the promisee does not affect the validity of the *stipulatio*.[14]

As long as the *stipulatio* existed, the position was always taken that it was valid, and the contractual action was not available even if the contract was entered into as a result of fraud, coercion, or error. In this regard, it is in stark contrast to the good-faith contracts, such as the consensual contracts of sale, hire, partnership, and mandate, which were coming into existence by the late third or early second century B.C.[15] But remedies for fraud were introduced by the praetor, Aquillius Gallus, probably when he was peregrine praetor in 66 B.C. He issued an edict that provided both an action for fraud, *actio de dolo*, and a defense of fraud, *exceptio doli*. His own definition of fraud, "When one thing is pretended, another done,"[16] shows there had to be dealings between the parties, that is, there had to be a contractual arrangement. That the *actio de dolo* was envisaged as a contractual, not delictal, remedy is confirmed by the fact that it lay only for the plaintiff's loss, not also for a penalty.[17] And the rule that the *actio de dolo* only lay where no other action was appropriate means that it could not have been issued for the good-faith contracts (where the relevant contractual action, as on sale, would lie), hence it was restricted to the strict law contracts, notably *stipulatio*.[18] The action would, therefore, lie when someone wished to recover what he had given under a *stipulatio* that he had been fraudulently induced to make.

More interesting in the present context is the defense of fraud that ran "if in this matter nothing has been done or is being done by the fraud of the plaintiff."[19] The position is that the plaintiff is bringing an action on the *stipulatio*, the defendant neither denies that he made the *stipulatio* nor that it is valid, but he has inserted into the pleadings a defense that means he will not be liable on the action if the plaintiff has acted or is acting fraudulently. The point is that fraud has not voided the *stipulatio* but will neutralize the action, provided the defendant promisor has the defense expressly inserted into the pleadings before *litis contestatio*, the joinder of issue.[20] The defendant will still lose if he omits the *exceptio doli*, and he cannot insert it into the pleadings after *litis contestatio*. Other remedies had been made available rather earlier, around 80 B.C., for the situation where a *stipulatio* was entered under duress.[21]

In the present inquiry the question inevitably arises whether the continued survival of a *stipulatio* entered into because of fraud, duress, or even error, and the continued power of the words used are to be understood as the result of the religious origins of the word used. The answer probably has to be in the negative. In the first place, it came early to be established that verbs other than *spondere* could be used to make a *stipulatio*, and these other verbs have no specific religious connotation.[22] Second, there is no indication that jurists were ever aware of the original, religious connotations of the verb *spondere*. Indeed, the notion of libation in the verb seems to be Indo-European rather than Latin, where *libare* was the verb used.[23]

We need see in this subsequent history of the *stipulatio* no more than the innate conservatism of the legal tradition. Often a rule or institution comes to exist with a clearly defined shape. Time may show that the rule or institution is inappropriate, but it may continue though surrounded by exceptions and qualifications.

One possibility, though, that we cannot exclude is that the verbal formality, the requirement of question and answer using the same verb, and the effectiveness of this with no relevance attached to the state of mind of the promisor, are the result of a frame of mind educated in the tradition of the nature of prayers and vows and of the interpretation of portents, first of the pontiffs, then of the jurists, who were steeped in their approach to legal reasoning. To the *stipulatio* we will return in the following chapter.

Mancipatio, the formal, verbal ceremony for transferring those kinds of property classed as *res mancipi*—namely, slaves, cattle, horses, mules and asses, rustic praedial servitudes, and Italic lands[24]—contains no feature that suggests that its formalism owes anything to Roman religion. For *res mancipi*, delivery (*traditio*) was not sufficient to transfer ownership, and a *mancipatio* was needed.[25] The form as it existed in classical law is described by Gaius.[26] In the presence of five adult Roman citizens who acted as witnesses, and of another who held a bronze scale, the transferee grasped the thing (except for land which could be mancipated at a distance), held a bronze ingot in his other hand, and said, "I declare this slave is mine according to the law of the citizens, and let him have been bought by me with this bronze and these bronze scales."[27] In early times there would be a weighing out of the bronze (or copper).

The ceremony of *mancipatio* was adapted pragmatically to a wide variety of uses: for the creation of rustic praedial servitudes (which were incorporeal); for the creation of marital power, *manus*, over a wife; for the adoption of a person in *patria potestas* (paternal power); for the creation of the form of real security called *fiducia;* for *nexum*, by which a free person was bound to a creditor; and for the making of a will, the *testamentum per aes et libram*.[28]

The history of *mancipatio* is therefore a great success story for legal opportunism. But it also shows that, although formalities, such as an oral declaration and the presence of the witnesses, were required, the wording was by no means fixed and rigid. For instance, for the *testamentum per aes et libram* the recipient, the *familiae emptor*, declared in early times something like "I declare your property to be subject to your instructions under my guardianship, so that you may lawfully make a will according to the public statute, and let it have been bought by me with this bronze and this bronze scale."[29] The practice of making such a will was confirmed by the Twelve Tables, though, until later, no heir could be appointed by it. Again, for *fiducia* the *mancipatio* contained words such as *fide et fiduciae*, showing that the ceremony was creating an interest based on reliance, hence a security, and that the recipient was obliged to use good faith. There is no indication that a mistake in the wording would prevent a *mancipatio* from being effective.

Mancipatio shows only that for the transfer of (what early came to be a fixed and limited class of) important property, publicity was needed for proof and that what was required for proof came to be fixed by law. In this regard, *mancipatio* has very similar analogues in the transfer of important property, especially land, in other systems. A good example is the necessity of delivery of sasine or livery of seisin in earlier English and Scottish land law.[30]

Likewise, we can infer nothing about the impact of religious verbal formalism on the words needed in testate succession for the institution of the heirs or for the creation of legacies. To the extent that formal words were needed, whether in an oral or a written will, the requirements correspond to that found elsewhere, where there has been no input from religion, for the initiation of an heir and for distinguishing the effects of one type of legacy from another.[31]

With regard to procedure there is a widely held view that in the archaic system of the *legis actiones* the precise strict wording had to be followed, or the party would lose his action. Kurt Latte, the expert on Roman religion, after maintaining that formalism in religious formulation was more pronounced and of longer duration among the Italians than it was in Greece, goes on: "Again there are expressions that are also to be found in the legal sphere: here too prevails the sentence that *ut vel qui minimum errasset, litem perderet* [that he who made the smallest mistake would lose his case] (G.4.30), here too is the solemn spoken word binding (Twelve Tables, 6.1, *uti lingua nuncupassit ita ius esto* [as the tongue spoke, so let the right be]). It is unjustified to seek for priority of one or the other use: rather, what is involved is a parallelism rooted in the unity of the manner of thinking."[32] Max Kaser, the Roman law scholar, claims: "The priestly coloration of the law reveals itself particularly in the strict binding force of form, which caused the legal act, just like the sacred act, to fail for the slightest error."[33] Such views are based on two texts of Gaius's *Institutes*.

> The actions which the old lawyers used were called *legis actiones*, actions of the law, either because they were produced by statute (because then praetorian Edicts, by which many actions have been introduced, were not used) or because they were framed in the very wording of the statutes themselves, and were therefore immutable, being observed as laws. Therefore, it was held that one who sued that his vines had been cut down, and named "vines" in his action, lost his case, because the law of the Twelve Tables, from which arose the action for cutting down vines, spoke generally of trees being cut down.[34]
>
> But all these *legis actiones* gradually became unpopular. For, from the over-subtlety of the old jurists who then built up the law, the matter was carried so far that whoever made the slightest mistake lost his case.[35]

But the standard view of verbal formalism is unacceptable. Against it, we have the magisterial words of David Daube.

> Among other methods of progress, interpretation—our main concern today—played a prominent part. In general, it followed sound lines from the outset, favouring a reasonable application of the code, neither too restrictive nor too broad. Thus, the rule of the XII Tables that, while the normal period of usucaption was one year, it was to be two years for land was extended to buildings, but not beyond buildings to, say, boats. This example shows that there was no difficulty about one kind of gap at least; namely, that resulting from the fact that the XII Tables might confine themselves to the most conspicuous case, without paying attention to other similar ones. Interpretation was fully capable of rectifying this "casuistic" bias of the code.
>
> A well-known illustration is furnished by the penalty of 25 coins imposed by the code for the cutting down of another man's tree. We are credibly informed of an occasion when somebody whose vines had been cut down claimed the fine. Had he referred to trees in this action, he would have won, but as he referred to vines, he

lost. Evidently, interpretation was sufficiently liberal to subsume vines under trees; what could not be admitted was the replacement of a statutory ground of action, the law concerning the destruction of a tree, by a fresh, non-statutory demand concerning the destruction of a vine.

The case is widely believed to reveal the ritualistic, magical character of the procedure of that epoch, with a slip of the tongue entailing irretrievable defeat. This view is mistaken. There is no question of a slip of the tongue. Plaintiff definitely rested his claim, not on the statute, but on what he considered a rational extension. In a system designed to provide security from arbitrary demands, it is quite understandable that the principle *nulla actio sine lege* should be jealously upheld. There is a great difference between allowing the law concerning the destruction of trees to cover that of vines—this the experts were prepared to do—and recognizing a new independent claim in respect of vines—this they refused to do. In the former case, the starting-point remains trees; once the starting point is vines, the claim could be extended to strawberries—25 coins a plant. It may not be accidental that the lawsuit in question was presumably between a well-to-do owner of a vineyard and a person of lesser standing. We may add that, though it is quite conceivable that at one time, in the *legis actio*, a slip of the tongue or a careless gesture was fatal, there is not a shred of evidence to this effect in the Roman sources.[36]

Daube's argument can be expanded. First, it should be noted that, as Daube says, Gaius nowhere writes of a slip of the tongue. It is not to be assumed that such an error, rather than the wrong formulation of a legal claim, caused the suit to be dismissed. But a slip of the tongue would vitiate a prayer. Second, the result of an error in a prayer vitiated the prayer, but the prayer could be repeated and be good. It is not plausible to maintain that a slip in verbal formalism in law would be treated more seriously—the action is gone forever—than in religion. Moreover, an unnoticed verbal slip in a *legis actio* could have no effect, whereas, as we have seen, it was the unnoticed error in a religious ritual that would be truly dangerous.

To conclude, verbal formalism is central to Roman religion, especially in prayers and vows. Verbal formalism plays a very restricted role in Roman law,[37] and to the extent that it does, this can scarcely be attributed to any connection between law and religion. Kaser insists that developed archaic Roman private law was in its essentials not sacred but priestly. He sees this priestly coloration in the law, as was mentioned, precisely in the strict binding force of form.[38] This strict binding force of form in early private law is greatly exaggerated. The priestly coloration has to be sought elsewhere.[39]

This conclusion has particular significance. Early Roman law was under the guidance of the pontiffs, who had control of the interpretation of the Twelve

Tables. Thus, formal acts and words, such as for *mancipatio,* for the institution of an heir, and for the *legis actiones,* were the creation of the pontiffs, at least in the sense that it was they who determined which form would have legal efficacy. Accordingly, it is very revealing that the pontiffs did not require for law the strict formalism that they did for religious acts. Law, as meant for plebeians, was a very different thing from acts that affected the disposition of the gods.

To restate the thesis of this chapter, the Romans were more relaxed about dealings between men than they were about dealings with gods. For the former they did not demand the formalism that they did for the latter.

5 *Votum* and *Stipulatio*

Scholars frequently postulate similarities with or connections between religious acts, such as *vota* (vows), prayers, sacrifices, and even treaties on the one hand, and private-law contracts on the other.

Vows seem to me to give the best arguments for similarities and connections, and we do have direct evidence for their form in the *acta fratrum Arvalium*, the records of the priesthood of the Arval brothers.[1] This priesthood appears to be ancient, but is usually thought to have died out in the republic, to be restored by Augustus.[2] Its early history can only be conjectured from (apparently) similar priesthoods elsewhere in early Italy.[3] But a considerable part of its records from the early empire have been recovered from the site where its cult acts were performed. The substantial fragments contain accounts of the formulation of the vows of the priesthood. Gaps in one vow can be reconstructed from others. The one printed here records a vow made on January 3, 81:

> Jupiter, Greatest and Best, if the Emperor Titus Caesar Vespasianus Augustus, chief priest, endowed with tribunician power, father of the country, and Caesar Domitianus, son of the deity, those whom we intend to name, live and (he) be safe at their home before 2 January next, for the Roman people and for the Roman state, and you keep that day and them safe from dangers if there are any or will have been any before that day, and you give a happy outcome, as we intend to state the same, and you keep them in the condition in which they now are or better, and you have done these things, then to you, in the name of the college of the Arval brotherhood, we vow there will be two golden oxen. Queen Juno, in the words in which we vowed two golden oxen to Jupiter, Greatest and Best, if you did those things we vow to you in the same words in the name of the college of the Arval brotherhood, two golden cows. Minerva, likewise. Public Safety, likewise.[4]

Whether the wording corresponds exactly to that of archaic vows of the Arval brotherhood cannot be directly established, but we can be fairly sure that it is close to earlier forms. In the first place, although this priesthood may have died out, other important ones did not, and they continued to make vows. In the second place, we do have Livy's account of a vow supposedly made in 217 B.C., and it shows similar features:

> When the senate had passed these resolutions, the praetor consulted the College of Pontiffs, and Lucius Cornelius Lentulus gave his opinion that a public vote had to be taken on the Sacred Spring: without the order of the people it could not be vowed. [2.] The question was put to the people in these words: "Do you will, and do you order these things to be done. If the state of the Roman people shall be preserved for the next five years—as I would wish it to be preserved—in these wars, namely the war of the Roman people with the Carthaginian, and the wars with the Gauls who are on this side of the Alps, [3.] let the Roman people offer as an indefeasible gift to be made to Jupiter, whatever the spring has produced of pigs, sheep, goats, and cattle, whatever has not been dedicated to another god, beginning from the day which the people and senate will have ordered. [4.] Whoever makes the sacrifice, let him make it whenever he wishes and by whatever rite he wishes. By whatever rite he makes it, let it be duly made. [5.] If an animal which should be sacrificed dies, let it be unconsecrate and let no guilt attach. If anyone injures or kills it unintentionally, let no guilt attach. If anyone steal it, let no guilt attach to the Roman people or to him from whom it was stolen. [6.] If he should sacrifice on a black day [i.e., one on which no public business should be transacted] unwittingly, let it be duly made. Let it be duly made, if made by night or day, if a slave or freeman made it. If the sacrifice is made before the senate and people ordered it to be made, let the people be absolved and free from obligation." [5]

We also have, from Macrobius, the forms of vows to persuade the deities to leave a besieged foreign city, and also to devote a foreign army or city to the deities. We need only quote the former.[6]

> Here is the formula by which the deities are brought out of a besieged city. "If it is a god, if it is a goddess, that has the people and state of Carthage under its protection, I beseech you, greatest one, I worship you [singular] who has taken over the protection of this city and people, and I request in mercy from you that you [plural] desert the people and state of Carthage, and remove yourselves from them; [8.] that you inject into that people and state, fear, terror, and oblivion, and that you come and transfer yourself to Rome, to me and mine; and that to you our territory, temples, holy things, and city will be more acceptable and more approved; and that you will be in command of me, the Roman people and my soldiers, in such a way that we know and understand this. If you will so have done, I vow I will dedicate to you temples and games." [7]

Although we have no surviving record of a private vow, the form for these would no doubt be similar.[8]

The vow involves a quid pro quo. The human binds himself to the performance of a specific act if the deity will act in a particular way. The curious thing is that, if we leave aside the early contract of *stipulatio* for the moment, no private-law contract equivalent to this existed in early law or in the classical scheme of contracts.

Roman law developed no general contract, apart from *stipulatio*, but only a system of individual contracts, each distinguished from one another by function or form. Strikingly, with three important and significant exceptions, they all had to be either unilateral or, of necessity, gratuitous. Unilateral were *mutuum* (loan for consumption), the contract *litteris*, and, of course, the *stipulatio* itself. Of necessity gratuitous were *commodatum* (loan for use), *depositum* (deposit), and *mandatum* (mandate). If payment in money was arranged for any of these three situations, then the contract in question would not arise, but a contract of hire (*locatio conductio*) would. If a nonmonetary reward was arranged, there would be no contract of *commodatum*, *depositum*, or *mutuum*, and there would be no contract of hire and no other contract either. The three exceptional contracts which were bilateral and not gratuitous were *emptio venditio* (sale), *locatio conductio* (hire), and *societas* (partnership). For sale and hire, the prestation on the one side always was to give coined money. They were, thus, the simplest possible bilateral, nongratuitous, contracts. *Societas* is an anomaly in various ways, arising out of the law of succession, and need not detain us here.[9]

What Roman law did not know, throughout the republic and even into the empire, was a specific contract that corresponded to what was substantively wanted in a vow. There was no contract for the performance of services in return for services or in return for goods. Admittedly, at some point not too far into the empire, barter (*permutatio*), delivery of goods in return for goods, emerged as an institution, but even so, and even in the time of Justinian, *permutatio* was never classed among the regular contracts.[10] The jurist Paul, of the late second and early third centuries A.D.,[11] shows that an action would lie in any of the following four situations: "I give that you give," *do ut des;* "I give that you do," *do ut facias;* "I do that you give," *facio ut des;* "I do that you do," *facio ut facias*.[12] On this basis, any bilateral agreement followed by performance by one party would allow that party to bring an action. But it will be noticed that the formulation of the vow has a very different stress: it is "You do that I give (or do)."

But, in actuality, the *votum* corresponds in great measure to the *stipulatio* of private law. I have argued elsewhere and for a different purpose that most of the Roman contracts, including *stipulatio*, give a distorted mirror effect to social relationships.[13] The *stipulatio* is presented as a formal, unilateral, contract; one party promises to the other, and the promisor alone is under an obligation. But no one usually makes a gratuitous promise by itself. Either a *stipulatio* is part of a continuing relationship where the parties have ongoing relations whether these are cast in legal form or not, or the legal obligation is met by a corresponding legal obligation. There are two scenarios for the latter eventuality. Either there are two *stipulationes,* one taken from each party, and these are made mutually dependent, or there is one *stipulatio,* but it is given by the party who will perform second, and it is conditional upon the prior performance by the other party. "If you pay me one hundred sesterces, I promise to deliver to you my horse called Seius." That is the secular contract that corresponds precisely to the *votum* to a god.[14]

There is, admittedly, a formal difference between the *votum* and the *stipulatio,* in that in the *votum* the promisee does not speak, but that is to be expected, given the nature of a vow. Even if deities were inclined to speak, they are not usually put in the position of claimants. Also, a deity should not be laying down the terms on which he will do something. The promisor makes his vow, and the deity may perform if he finds the vow adequate. Despite what has just been said, however, there is some indication that in prayer a god might be asked to promise. Under *bene sponsis,* Festus, *On the Meaning of Words,* has: "Messalla, the augur, says that 'Have you promised faithfully, and Have you faithfully purposed' in the augural prayer means 'Have you promised, Have you purposed.' "[15] If in the remote past *stipulatio* had origins in religion, as was suggested in the preceding chapter, and if it became the private law analogue to the vow, then the *votum* may help to explain peculiarities of the *stipulatio.*

Thus, an origin in religion would make more comprehensible the fact that originally only one verb, *spondere,* was allowed to make a binding *stipulatio.* It was not enough to respond in the same verb, "I give"; the notion of a promise must be expressed. It could also help to explain why it was the oldest type of contract, no other being actionable.

A connection with *votum* would, however, not explain why the *stipulatio* had to be oral; orality as a formality is to be expected in archaic times, given the scarcity of writing. But a connection with *votum*—even one forgotten but which had stamped the concept of *stipulatio*—would help to explain why it never came subsequently to be accepted that *stipulatio* could be made in writing without the use of spoken words.[16] It would also help to explain *stipulatio* as *the* Roman contract, all the others (with the exception of *societas*) arising to meet situations where a *stipulatio* was inappropriate, difficult, or impossible.[17]

Further, the rigid attitude in *stipulatio*, laying great stress on the words used—the promisor is taken to mean what he says, and only what he says—is paralleled in the *votum*.[18] In the *vota* already quoted, one even sees protective phrases: "those whom we mean to name" (*quos nos sentimus dicere*); "as we intend to say" (*ita uti nos sentimus dicere*); "as I would wish it preserved" (*sicut velim eam salvam*); and again, "however he does it, let it be properly done" (*quo modo faxit, probe factum esto*); "if it be a god, if it be a goddess" (*si deus si dea est*).

It should also be noticed that *votum* shares in the legal terminology of *stipulatio*. Cicero writes of the *votis sponsio, qua obligamur deo,* "The *sponsio* of a vow, by which we are under an obligation to a god."[19] Macrobius claims "haec vox propria sacrorum est, ut reus vocetur qui suscepto voto se numinibus obligat" (This is the technical term in sacrifices: he who binds himself to the gods by a vow is called *reus*, debtor).[20] *Reus* is also the technical term for the debtor in *stipulatio*.[21]

In many situations, moreover, the *stipulatio* that one wanted would be very complicated, subject to conditions, and difficult to frame.[22] It is very likely the familiarity with the complexities of *vota* that enabled jurists to deal with such a *stipulatio* and contributed to its continued popularity.

Prayers, sacrifices, and treaties were formulaic, with the same characteristics as *vota*.[23] But we need not examine them here.

6 The Oath in Private Law

The use made of oaths in a legal system should be particularly instructive in evaluating the interaction of law and religion.

The oath may be given widespread or limited recognition. It may be held legally appropriate only when some other religious issue is involved. It may relate to past acts, existing facts, or future conduct. When it relates to past acts or existing facts, it may be tested by supernatural or secular means. The penalty for falsely swearing an oath may be sacral or secular.

In fact, the oath plays a limited, but fascinating, role in Roman private law. It appears to have legal consequences in only four contexts, three of these concerning procedure. One of these three, the form of action known as the *legis actio sacramento*, is very old.

The *legis actio sacramento* was expressly mentioned in the Twelve Tables. Some scholars, indeed, believe it is the most archaic of the *legis actiones*.[1] It was also a general action in the sense that it was used in circumstances for which no other action had been provided by law. This does not mean, of course, that it may not also have been given by statute for specific cases.

The *legis actio sacramento* could be brought either *in rem* or *in personam*. The former version—which alone need be discussed here, since for our purposes the *actio in personam* is essentially similar—can be reconstructed, thanks to Gaius's *Institutes* 4.13–17. The first party claimed: "I affirm that this slave is mine by the law of the citizens according to his proper title. As I have declared, look, I have laid my staff on him." At the same time he laid his rod (*festuca*) on the slave. The second party then said and did the same. The praetor intervened, saying, "Both let go the slave." The first party then said, "I ask, will you say on what title you made your claim?" The other: "I exercised my right by laying on my staff." The first party again: "Since you have claimed wrongfully, I challenge you by an oath (*sacramentum*) of 500 asses."[2] The opponent likewise said "And I you."

Some elements in this remain obscure, but most of the difficulties need not concern us. For example, it is not clear that the rod is to be regarded as Gaius states as a symbol for a spear. It may be nothing more than the stick that farmers (and others) frequently carry and use to control beasts, as a pointer, as a stick to lean on, and so on.[3] Again, the words *secundum suam causam* may be linked conceptually either to the preceding or to the subsequent words. Certainty is not possible.[4]

After the procedure described, the subsequent stages of the action continued on the issue of the veracity of the oath, and the verdict was that a *sacramentum* was *iniustum,* false. The veracity of the oath, of course, depended on which party actually was owner of the slave, and the verdict on the oath thus in fact decided who was to get the slave. What matters here is that the action was general in the sense that it could be used whenever no other action had been provided. That is to say that the device of an action on the veracity of the oath was to enable litigation of a secular issue for which no action was provided. Thus, the purpose of the oath was entirely secular. But more than that, no magic or intervention of a deity was then involved in deciding whether the oath was correctly or falsely sworn.[5] The truth or otherwise of the oath depended entirely on the secular facts at issue, and the secular law applied to them. The oath simply enabled the trial to proceed with an examination of the facts by men. Still more, there was no divine sanction for breach of the oath—there was only the secular loss of the penalty.[6] This is a world away from the medieval trial by ordeal.[7]

It may well be—I have no intention of investigating the issue—that in remote antiquity the forerunner of the *legis actio sacramento* did operate in a sacred way, in a narrow range of circumstances, with the false oath supposedly bringing the wrath of a deity, and the deposited money being a sin offering, *piaculum*.[8] If this was so, then it is all the more significant that it disappeared without leaving any trace in the record, to be supplanted with such a secular action as the *legis actio sacramento*.[9]

The one instance in substantive law where an oath was accorded legal recognition was the *iusiurandum liberti*, the oath of a freedman. This is so exceptional that Gaius, in a defective text, remarks on its uniqueness, and apparently contrasts Roman law in this regard with other systems.[10] The background is this. Often when a master freed a slave, he would want the freedman to perform services for him for a number of days per year. To ensure that the freedman would perform, the master could take a *stipulatio* to that effect from him, immediately following the manumission. But the problem was that the slave, once freed, might simply refuse to give the *stipulatio* and there was no means to compel him. This difficulty could not be solved by the owner taking a *stipulatio* from the slave before manumission. The problem was that there could be no contract between an owner and his slave.[11] The solution was for the slave to give an oath before he was freed, and this put him under a religious obligation to renew his promise, after manumission, usually by another oath, though a *stipulatio* was possible. This second oath, which is the *iusiurandum liberti*, was then a formal verbal civil-law obligation, though the oath made while the man was a slave did not constitute a legal obligation.[12] A text of Venuleius is informative: "Although it was previously doubted whether only a slave or a freedman[13] by swearing an oath was bound to a patron for those burdens imposed on account of freedom, nonetheless the truer opinion is that he is not bound except as a free person. But it is on that account that it is usual to exact an oath from slaves so that bound by religion, after they become their own master, they are under the necessity of swearing an oath, provided that as soon as he is freed he swears or promises."[14] Thus, the freedman's oath creates a private-law obligation and that is its purpose. It is very secular. It is used to circumvent a difficulty of private law that could not otherwise be solved.

Much is obscure about the *iusiurandum liberti*. We do not know how early the private-law action was granted on the freedman's oath. It is not evidenced before the empire, though at least by the late second century B.C. an oath was being taken from the slave, then was followed by another oath on manumission.[15] We do not know the nature of the religious obligation to give another oath or promise on manumission. We do not know why before the time of Venuleius (who was active about the middle of the second century A.D.) the question existed as to whether the slave's oath could create a legal obligation. It is even uncertain why the freedman gave an oath rather than (as he also could) a *stipulatio*. Presumably, owners in practice often took an oath from the freedman, not an enforceable stipulation, and at some time the oath was reinforced by a private-law action. What really matters in the present context is that the purpose of the one oath that is functional in substantive law is purely secular and gives rise to secular consequences—namely, the private-law action.

To return to procedure. Another procedural oath, the *iusiurandum in litem*, is perhaps particularly significant in this context. It is a marked feature of Roman law that the award, *condemnatio*, in an action was always a sum of money. At times, though, what the plaintiff really wanted, and was reasonable for him to have, was something other than money, such as the object of the dispute. This could not be directly achieved by the *condemnatio*. Then, for a number of actions,[16] the instructions to the *iudex* might contain the so-called *clausula arbitraria* to order actual restitution to his satisfaction, and to condemn only if this order was disobeyed.[17] The order for restitution could not be directly enforced. But if restitution was not forthcoming, the judge could condemn by his own estimation of value or he could proffer the oath, the *iusiurandum in litem* to the plaintiff to state the value.

The texts on *iusiurandum in litem* tell a remarkably consistent and coherent—if apparently unlikely—story.

First, the plaintiff is allowed to swear the oath as to value if the defendant is malicious, fraudulent, or contumacious but not if the defendant has simply been negligent. Thus,

> Whether we sue for something as our own or that it be produced, sometimes only the interest of the plaintiff is estimated, as when someone's negligence in not restoring or producing is penalized. But when it is a case of someone's malice or contumacy in not restoring or producing, then what holds is the plaintiff's oath as to value.[18]

> But in all these actions the oath as to value is taken only on account of fraud, not also of negligence. That the judge estimates.[19]

Second, the texts declare, more or less expressly, that the amount sworn to in the oath is not expected to be the same as the true valuation, and that, nonetheless, the condemnation will then be for the amount of the oath. Thus,

> We do not consider that a matter brought into court goes up on that account, namely, that the condemnation can increase because of the contumacy of a defendant who will not restore through an *iusiurandum in litem*. For the matter does not thereby go up in value, but because of the contumacy an estimation is made beyond the value of the matter.[20]

Third, the texts declare quite expressly that powers exist in the judge to restrain the plaintiff from setting the valuation just too blatantly high. Thus,

> There is no limit to the amount that can be set in an oath. But I ask whether a judge can set a measure to the oath so that it be within a certain amount, lest one seizes the occasion to swear in an immense sum? And, indeed, it is settled that it is in the discretion of the judge to withhold the oath. Therefore, the question really is whether he who can withhold the oath can fix a limit to the amount of the oath. This is in accord with the discretion of the judge, which is based on good faith.[21]

Fourth, and most surprising, we even have a text that frankly states: "It is not readily allowed to inquire into the perjury of one who swears the oath of value under necessity of law."[22]

Thus, to achieve the very secular purpose of compelling a fraudulent or contumacious defendant to specific performance, which was not directly possible in Roman law, resort could be had to an oath put to the plaintiff to estimate the amount of his claim. And the plaintiff was in fact expected to exaggerate. The account in the texts, so well documented and consistent as it is, seems so surprising that Fritz Schulz claims: "This *iusiurandum in litem* was an expedient designed to hasten condemnation, as it spared the judge a wearisome and lengthy task. The idea was not to compel the defendant to make specific restitution by threatening him with an assessment made by the plaintiff himself, who might considerably exceed the real value. Modern historians as usual underrate Roman *fides* and piety. To be sure the Roman principle was *deorum iniuria diis curae* [an injury to the gods is the concern of the gods], but even an average Roman did not forswear himself lightly."[23] Alas, Schulz cannot be correct.[24] The *iusiurandum in litem* indicates that the Roman deities did not object to their names being taken in vain.[25]

The remaining use of the oath in procedure has nothing remarkable about it and we need not linger over it. There is a parallel in modern French law. In some actions before asking for his *formula*—that is, the form of pleadings—the plaintiff might proffer an oath to the defendant on the truth of the essentials of his case. If the defendant swore in the words put to him, the plaintiff lost his case. If he refused, the defendant lost his case. If he offered the oath back to the plaintiff, the similar alternatives existed.[26] The whole point of this oath was to shorten proceedings.[27] If a person was seen to be foresworn he was subjected to a beating.[28]

Thus, only in very limited circumstances was the oath given legal recognition in Roman private law. In all cases, the oath was used for secular purposes, and the only penalty for swearing falsely in the *legis actio sacramento* or in the *iusiurandum necessarium* or for failing to perform after the *iusiurandum liberti* was equally secular. Strikingly, in three of the four instances the oath was a dodge or device to bypass a problem that was posed by the logic of secular law.

The use of the oath in Roman private law is a fine example of what I want to call "second best and the law."[29] Often a person with a law job to do has a dilemma. There is nothing satisfactory that he or she can do, but something ought to be done. For instance, frequently a judge does not know what to decide, but he or she is nowhere permitted to render the judgment "I do not know." At times, the law allows for concessions in such a quandary. It permits use to be made of "the second best." But the dodge, the cop-out, cannot be admitted—that would injure the gravity of the law. The court cannot say, "To resolve our perplexity, we leave everything to chance. Let us throw dice." Instead, the cop-out, the figurative throwing of the dice, is imbued with particular solemnity.

I am, of course, not attributing bad faith to the inventors of the second best. They are doing the best they can in the face of a serious problem. What reveals to the outsider a recourse to a procedure as an instance of the second best is precisely that it is not always used where the outsider would expect it, but exactly where a cop-out was needed. Legal historians must be on the lookout for the second best because it will always appear in its society with enhanced significance. It is likely to mislead because its actual significance is not that which appears on the face of the procedure.

To illustrate this notion for our purposes we may look at a quasi-legal institution, the formal, official, or even ritual, curse with a religious backing which is used when a legal wrong has been committed. This type of curse has a long history, but it is used only in very limited circumstances: namely, where the wrongdoer cannot be established; where the wrongdoer is beyond reach either because he or she cannot be found or is too powerful; and less often, where it cannot be proven that the suspected crime actually occurred. An illuminating example occurs in the Bible at Numbers 5.11ff. In certain circumstances when a husband accused his wife of adultery, the priest would utter a curse upon her if she had sworn falsely, and (after she had drunk the water of contention) she would (in theory) have a miscarriage if her oath was falsely sworn. God, who established this procedure, was quite specific about the circumstances in which it could be used: only when the husband was very jealous but direct evidence was lacking. In view of the familial discord some resolution of the dispute was needed, but there was a complete impasse until this device was created.

What we do not find in the history of such formal curses is their application to the accused after guilt has been established. But why not? It surely seems appropriate that a heinous wrongdoer be condemned after conviction to suffer punishment by God as well as by man. And it would add to the solemnity of the punishment. The explanation in the general case is that the formal curse is not used as punishment because it is not needed. The curse is used when the guilty party is beyond the reach of the law. It is resorted to as the "second best," the best that can be done in the circumstances. In all this I am not suggesting bad faith on the part of those who introduced the curse. The feeling is not that the deity involved does not hear or that there is no deity. Rather, the notion is that the deity may not act. The deity does not always intervene. So the cursing is reserved for situations where no other solution would help, but action is required. What outsider scholars must not do when investigating an alien society is to say: "Formal cursing is accepted and approved by the society. That means the society has complete faith in divine intervention."

To return to the use of the oath in Roman law. The second-best nature is revealed for *iusiurandum liberti* in that it was not possible without the oath from the slave to create a binding obligation (unless the slave was subsequently willing), and in that an oath was not permitted legal impact in other contracts; for the *legis actio sacramento* in that the action was available where no other was provided, and in that an oath had no legal role in other actions; for *iusiurandum in litem* in that no other way was available to compel specific performance, that it was allowed only against a contumacious or fraudulent defendant, and that it was not easily subject to an action for perjury. The formality should not mislead us into believing great Roman reliance on religion for the law.

7   The Pontiffs and the Family

In three distinct contexts, changing the family relationship necessitated the involvement of the pontiffs: entering a marriage with *manus* by *confarreatio;* adoption by *adrogatio;* appointing an heir by will *calatis comitiis*. Yet, one could also enter a marriage *cum manu*, adopt, or make a will by other modes that did not involve the pontiffs. Indeed, in these other modes no religious intervention was needed at all and, if it did occur, would have no legal consequences.

As early as the making of the Twelve Tables there were two kinds of Roman marriage: with *manus* (*cum manu*) and without *manus* (*sine manu*). In the former, the wife ceased to belong to her original family and became legally a member of the husband's family, subject to the power (*manus*) of the head of the family, whether that was her husband or an ascendant of his. In the latter, the wife did not legally become a member of her husband's family but remained in her original family subject to the *patria potestas* of her father or grandfather, or was free of power, *sui iuris*, if they were dead.

Manus could be created in three ways, all of which also existed in the time of the Twelve Tables. Only *confarreatio* was a religious ceremony. *Coemptio* was a variant form of *mancipatio:* in appearance the husband "bought" the wife. By *usus* a woman in a marriage *sine manu* came into the *manus* of her husband or his *pater* after a year unless she had stayed away from home for three nights.[1]

The central part of *confarreatio* was a sacrifice to Jupiter Farreus of bread made with spelt (*far*), fruits of the earth, and salt cake, with the assistance of both the *pontifex maximus* and the flamen Dialis, and in the presence of ten witnesses.[2] Formal words were required but we do not know who spoke them.[3]

At the time of the Twelve Tables, the *rex sacrorum* was the leading priest, only subsequently to be displaced by the *pontifex maximus*, and both of them, as we have seen, had to be patricians.[4] Even at that time, the *pontifex maximus* was a leading citizen. In these circumstances, especially given the importance and heavy duties of the flamen Dialis and *pontifex maximus*, *confarreatio* cannot have been an everyday occurrence and in practice would be restricted to patricians.[5] It may be observed that the *rex sacrorum*, the flamen Dialis, the flamen Martialis, and the flamen Quirinalis had to be married by *confarreatio*, and be born of parents so married.[6]

Whether *confarreatio* was mentioned in the Twelve Tables is a matter of doubt. Probably the majority of scholars would hold that it was not, though I have argued to the contrary. The brief argument is that we have four texts, not all of which are obviously historically connected, that have the phrase *usu, farre(o), coemptione*.[7] This can only be a list of the ways of creating *manus*. The order is always the same (and it cannot be the order of historical emergence), the nouns are always in the ablative, and *farre* is used instead of *confarreatio*. The similarities of form are such that the texts must go back to a common source which was well known and authoritative, and this can only mean legislation. The only possible legislation would be the Twelve Tables.[8] If this view is correct, then its present significance lies in the position of *usus* at the head of the list, although *usus* must have been the last of the three to emerge. I would then put this together with the prominence of clauses on *usus*, long use, in general in the Twelve Tables to postulate that not only was *usus* an innovation for the acquisition of ownership, so also was it for the acquisition of *manus* in marriage. The provision, then, was primarily about *usus*. That is to say, in my view *confarreatio* was mentioned only incidentally in the Twelve Tables. For other scholars it was not mentioned at all, which would be even more significant.[9]

In the last century of the republic, *manus* marriage disappeared, really because it was no longer wanted.[10] *Confarreatio* would in any event have ceased, because between 87 B.C. and Augustus no flamen Dialis was appointed.[11] Augustus restored *confarreatio*, but only with religious effect.

Adoption in the shape of *adrogatio* also existed at the time of the Twelve Tables. Though we are not well informed of it for the fifth century B.C., we have a clear picture of it from the first century B.C., when it was the form of adoption for a male *sui iuris*. It would, thus, entail the destruction of a Roman family, and was permitted only if otherwise the family of the adopter would die out. *Adrogatio* was in two stages. First, its advisability was inquired into by the pontiffs. If they approved, the matter went before the *comitia calata*, which was summoned by the *pontifex maximus*. The adopter and adoptee were asked if they approved, then a *rogatio*, a question if the people so wished and ordered, was put to the assembled populace. The *adrogatio* was thus a legislative act in the *comitia calata*. Since only males could appear in the *comitia calata*, only males could be adrogated, and in all probability they would have to be above puberty.[12]

Adrogatio was the only form of adoption existing at the time of the Twelve Tables. *Adoptio*, which was the form used in later law for the adoption of persons in *patria potestas*, resulted from a deliberate misinterpretation of the Twelve Tables, hence it has to be later than that code. There is no evidence that *adrogatio* was mentioned in the Twelve Tables.

Although we have no textual information, it is safe to assume that *adrogatio* in practice at least was very much restricted to a small section of the upper classes. It did, after all, require not only a pontifical investigation but also legislation.[13] A difference from *confarreatio* ought to be noted. In *confarreatio* it was the religious ceremony that made the marriage and conferred the *manus*. In *adrogatio*, it was the vote of the people that created the adoption.

The *testamentum calatis comitiis* died out very early, and the surviving information is so sparse that one cannot be sure it should be discussed in this context.[14] It was a true will, involving the appointment of an heir, made in the *comitia calata*, which met twice each year on March 24 and May 27 for this purpose. It was, thus, very public, a disadvantage that, together with the limited times when it could be made, ensured its demise.

The *comitia calata* was, of course, summoned by the *pontifex maximus*, but whether there was an investigation into the advisability of the will cannot be determined. Nor do we know whether the assembled people simply acted as witnesses or concluded a legislative act. It is frequently suggested that the testator could make a will only if he had no *suus heres*, that is, someone who would become free of paternal power on his death, hence the purpose of the will would be to allow the rites of his family cult to be continued. It has even been conjectured that this will was originally an adoption by *adrogatio*, whose effects were delayed until the death of the *adrogans*.[15] But there is no real evidence. Given the intervention of the *comitia calata* here, I would, however, believe there was a significant role for the pontiffs.

There is no evidence that the *testamentum comitiis calatis* was dealt with in the Twelve Tables. Another form of will, the *testamentum per aes et libram*, was confirmed by the code, though I believe that only at a later period could an heir be appointed under it.[16] The *testamentum per aes et libram* was entirely secular.

In this case, too, it seems that we have one will that was in practice very much restricted to the upper classes and involved the intervention of the state and of the state religion, and another will that was widely available and was totally removed from the sphere of the state religion.

The first observation to be made on the foregoing is that where the state religion was involved in producing legal consequences for a family, the involvement was restricted to patricians or, at best, a very small section of the upper classes. Otherwise, for marriage, adoption, and will making, there was no involvement of state religion. More than that, in such spheres as *coemptio* and *usus* (for *manus*), *adoptio,* and the *testamentum per aes et libram,* no religious act had any legal consequences. We know that religious ceremonies were usual in the celebration of Roman marriages,[17] but except for *confarreatio,* these were neither legally necessary nor validating. We must conclude that the leaders of state religion and law were little concerned to inject religion into the family life of the great majority of Roman citizens.[18]

A second observation is that *confarreatio* is mentioned only incidentally, if at all, in the Twelve Tables; *adrogatio* and the *testamentum calatis comitiis* are apparently mentioned not at all. In contrast, the acquisition of *manus* by *usus* seems to be at the root of the clause that mentions *confarreatio,* and the *testamentum per aes et libram* is specifically confirmed. There are several possible explanations. First, that *confarreatio, adrogatio,* and the *testamentum calatis comitiis* were so well established that there was no need to spell out the law. Second, that they concerned only patricians, and the Twelve Tables were giving the law fit for plebeians. Third, that they involved the state religion, and that was basically excluded from the codification. I would tend to give weight to the first two suggestions, which are not incompatible.

8 Religion and Property

Writing around the middle of the second century A.D., Gaius claims: "Thus, the principal division of things is into two classes: for some are subject to divine law, others to human law. [3] Subject to divine law are *res sacrae* and *res religiosae*. [4] *Res sacrae* are those consecrated to the gods above, *res religiosae* are those dedicated to the gods of the underworld."[1] The conditions for things becoming subject to divine law, and the legal relationship of such things to human law, cast a particularly bright light on Roman legal and religious thought.

Property, whether a building or moveable, became *sacer* only when it was consecrated by individuals properly authorized by the Roman state or people to do so. Cicero says: "For I see there is an ancient law enacted by a tribune that forbids a building, land, or altar to be consecrated without popular mandate."[2] Livy, writing about the activities of the curule aedile Gnaeus Flavius in 304 B.C., and the hostility occasioned by them, related, "And so, in accordance with a resolution of the senate, a measure was enacted by the people that no one might dedicate a temple or altar without the authorization of the senate or a majority of the tribunes of the plebs."[3] This occurred after the *pontifex maximus* had claimed that by custom only the consul or general could dedicate a temple.[4]

And, as we have already seen in chapter 1, Cicero, reporting the judgment of the pontiffs on whether his house had been properly consecrated as a temple, gives as the wording, "If the person claiming to have dedicated had not been appointed by name either by order of the people or by a decree of the plebs, and if he had not been commanded to do so by an order of the people or decree of the plebs, then it appeared that that part of the site might be restored to me without sacrilege."[5] In the empire the jurist Gaius says that, to be sacred, land had to be consecrated by authority of the people—for instance, by a statute or resolution of the senate.[6]

There may have been dispute as to which public body or official could make property *sacer*—later, only the emperor could make property *sacer*⁷—or the rules may have changed from time to time, but it is beyond dispute that a private citizen by dedicating to a deity property, such as part of his land, or an altar on his land, could not make it *sacer*.⁸ The effect of property becoming *sacer* was that it was removed from human commerce, it could not be usucapted,⁹ and if it was taken away wrongfully the wrongdoer did not commit the private-law delict of theft (*furtum*) but the crime of sacrilege (*sacrilegium*).¹⁰

The texts on *res sacrae* again bring out the very close connection of the Roman state with Roman religion. Public bodies, public officials who are not pontiffs, can consecrate property (if they have proper authority) to the gods, with legal effect. Private citizens cannot.¹¹ Indeed one must go further:

> When Licinia, a Vestal Virgin, of noble birth and distinguished by the most holy priesthood, dedicated in the consulship of Titus Flaminius and Quintus Metellus, an altar, an oratory, and a sacred couch, did not the praetor, Sextus Julius, on the senate's authority, refer the issue to that college? Then the *pontifex maximus*, Publius Scaevola, responded on behalf of the college: "That which Licinia, daughter of Gaius, dedicated in a public place without the order of the people is not considered sacred."¹²

The events related occurred in 123 B.C. Thus, even a Vestal Virgin—and they were at least closely associated with the College of Pontiffs—could not make property *sacer*. The capacity to render things sacred was reserved to the state and not granted even to the state priests. A prior paragraph of Cicero, *De domo sua* 53.136, records a *responsum* of the *pontifex maximus* Marcus Aemilius that a censor could not dedicate a statue to Concord unless the people gave him express authority to do so, so that he was acting on their instructions.

The law on *res religiosae* is significant in a different way.¹³ *Res religiosae* were nothing but tombs, and they became consecrated only when a body was buried by someone who had the right to bury a body there. Such a person was usually the owner; indeed Gaius says: "On the other hand, we make a place *religiosus* by burying a dead body in our land, provided his funeral is our responsibility."¹⁴ Thus, though the question was posed, the general opinion was that, if one of the co-owners of land buried a body in the jointly owned land, he did not make it *religiosus*.¹⁵ Cicero records that the College of Pontiffs decreed that public land could not be made *religiosus* by a private act: hence many graves found in a public place were dug up.¹⁶ But when the owner of land buried a body in it, when it was appropriate for him to see to the funeral, the land became *religiosus*, even though the body was that of a slave.¹⁷

It was the College of Pontiffs who decided what was required to make the land *religiosus*—not before the sacrifice of a pig, says Cicero, and in the case of cremation, not before turf was placed on the bones—and what was required to make the deceased's family free from defilement.[18] The legalistic character of Roman religion determined that to make a tomb *religiosus* it was not enough for a body (or the ashes) to be buried there with proper rites: the person who carried out the burial must have had a right to bury in that place, and to be properly responsible for burying that body.

The legalistic approach to religious property is well brought out in a text that concerns both *res sacrae* and *res religiosae*. "When places are captured by enemies, everything ceases to be religious or sacred (just as free men are thus brought into slavery). But if they are released from this calamity, they are restored to their previous status as if they had returned with a kind of *postliminium*."[19] The text is, of course, concerned with Roman law. When Roman territory was captured by an enemy it ceased to be Roman. Property consecrated to Roman gods ceased to be sacred, and tombs made *religiosus* by the acts of individuals lost their religious status. What the position might be under the law of the conquering power was irrelevant to the jurists. The text comes from Pomponius's commentary on Quintus Mucius and at least the first part of the text will go back to the earlier jurist. *Postliminium* was, in short, the right by which under particular circumstances a Roman who had lost his citizenship— for instance, by capture in war—regained it and some other personal rights by returning to Roman territory. *Postliminium* also applied in the late republic to slaves and some other kinds of property.[20] It would not be anomalous for *postliminium* to apply to land, but there is no way to determine whether the second part of the text corresponds to the law of Quintus Mucius's time or is an addition by Pomponius. In either event, it is also instructive for Roman legal attitudes to religion.

9 State Religion and Alien Religion

The Roman state and Roman religion were intertwined. The gods protected and strengthened the state. The priests were public officials who performed the rites that the gods wished or required. If the rites were not duly performed, the gods were under no obligation to protect the state. Piety was not usually required, whether from priest or private citizen,[1] but performance of the rites was. On this approach, what has to be stressed is the utility of religion to the state.[2] That utility would be apparent even to Romans who were unconvinced of the complete validity of the religion. Since welfare of the state easily slides into the welfare of the leading citizens in the estimate of these leaders, it is not hard for us on this basis to comprehend manipulation of the religion to favor the interests of those in power.[3] Even private religion or cults were the business of the state. Only those established by long usage were acceptable.

This picture of Roman religion entails a very conservative approach. The customs of the ancestors, which seemed to have been rewarded by the approval of the gods, were revered. Innovations were distrusted. This explains the attitude to foreign cults, which otherwise appears contradictory. The Romans could be and were tolerant of other religions, especially well-established religions, outside of Rome and among non-Romans, including those of conquered people and even in the provinces,[4] except where such religions were overtly dangerous or hostile to Roman religion or the Roman state. With regard to foreign cults at Rome or among Romans, only one of two official responses was possible. Either the foreign religion or ritual was accepted by the state and incorporated as part of the official religion, or the foreign performance of the religion itself was declared to be criminal, independently even of excesses associated with it. Both approaches have a long history at Rome. Which was accepted depended upon the times and the nature of the religion. A third approach, to ignore the foreign worship, could be maintained for a period if the times were peaceable, the worship apparently innocuous, and its adherents few.

The traditional approach to religion found expression in various contexts.

Thus, Cicero, giving what he regards as the ideal religious laws for a state, summarizes the Roman attitudes.

> They are to approach the gods in purity, showing piety [*pietas*], leaving riches. Whoever acts otherwise, the god himself will deal out punishment.
>
> No one may have gods to himself, whether they are new gods or foreign gods, unless they have been accepted by the state. Privately they are to worship in accordance with the cults they have received from their ancestors. . . .
>
> They are to preserve the rites of their family and their ancestors.
>
> They are to worship as gods both those who have always been regarded as divine and those whose merits have placed them in heaven, Hercules, Liber, Aesculapius, Castor, Pollux, Quirinus: and those qualities on account of which ascent to heaven is granted to mankind, Intellect, Virtue, Piety, Good Faith. To their praise are to be shrines, but none to vices.
>
> They are to perform the established rites.[5]

Cicero then lists the obligations for holidays, the offices of pontiffs, flamines, and vestal virgins, sacrifices, auguries, and so on.

It is, of course, quite remarkable but utterly Roman to set out, as Cicero does, a religion as a code of law. It is equally remarkable that, as we know from other sources, the setting up of altars and temples and their appropriate rites were the subject of precise legislation.[6] Likewise, Aulus Gellius's account of the vestal virgins in *Noctes Atticae* 1.12 is purely a statement of law that significantly derives from the jurist Antistius Labeo.

To return to the quotation from Cicero: it is also noteworthy that he says nothing about any obligation to believe in the gods and nothing about theology. Certainly he says that one is to bring *pietas* to the gods, but that is linked with leaving gifts; which element is more important is not clear. Moreover, Roman *pietas* is not the same as our piety.[7] Cicero, indeed, himself defines it as that "which admonishes us to do our duty to our country, or our parents or our other blood relations"; and he contrasts it with *religio*, which consists "in the fear and reverence of the gods."[8] It is to be observed, moreover, that a breach of the duty here is left to the god to punish, no human penalty being prescribed. This is in contrast to penalties set down in subsequent sections of Cicero's religious code: thus, the same penalty that is established for parricide is to be imposed for theft of what is sacred or is entrusted to what is sacred; the penalty of disgrace (*dedecus*) for perjury; capital punishment inflicted by the pontiffs for sex with a vestal virgin; and an unspecified penalty for not performing a vow scrupulously.

Cicero also stresses that no one is to have private gods, unless such have been recognized by the state. Private cults are to be observed as they were by the ancestors. But he also shows that new gods can be accepted, such as Hercules and Liber (or Bacchus). In this context, Festus's definition of religious people is instructive: "They are called religious (*religiosi*) who have chosen to fulfill or pass over religious observances in accordance with the custom of the state, and who do not involve themselves with alien cults (*superstitiones*)."[9]

Other Roman writers illustrate the same approach to deities not recognized by the state. According to Livy, in the later fifth century B.C. there was a severe drought, followed by an epidemic:

> Nor was it bodies alone that were infected by disease, but there were many kinds of superstition, especially foreign; and that sort of person who can turn others' superstitious fears to their own advantage introduced new rites of sacrifice and prophecies into homes, [10.] until the public debasement came to the notice of the leaders of the state. They could not but notice in every street and chapel foreign and unusual offerings to beseech the peace of the gods. [11.] The task was then given to the aediles to see to it that none except Roman gods were worshipped, and only in the traditional manner.[10]

Given the bareness of Roman official religion, it cannot be a cause of surprise that in times of trouble and disaster Romans turned in their despair to foreign gods and rites.[11] These gods and rites were not recognized by the state, which then, according to Livy, intervened to ensure by law that only accepted Roman gods were worshipped and then only in the established manner. What is doubly significant in this account of Livy is that the coercion needed to bring this about was entrusted not to religious officials such as the pontiffs, but to the aediles, who were the elected secular officials in charge of the streets and markets.[12] In passing, it may be noticed that this intertwining of the official religion with the Roman state is typical. It is entirely in keeping that when a Vestal Virgin died intestate her property did not go to the temple of Vesta, but to the state.[13]

For the year 212 B.C., during the war with Hannibal, Livy records very similar events. Women, especially, were praying and sacrificing in new ways, and new priests and prophets appeared.[14] The senate censured the aediles and police magistrates for their failure to control the city, and these officials themselves scarcely escaped rough treatment from the crowd when they tried to clear the forum:

> When the evil appeared to be too great to be calmed by minor magistrates, the senate entrusted to Marcus Aemilius the urban praetor, the task of releasing the people from these superstitions. [12.] He recited the decree of the senate at a mass meeting

and pronounced that whoever had books of prophecies or prayers or of sacrificial rituals was to bring all such written material to him before the first of April; and that no one should sacrifice in a public or sacred place by a new or foreign ritual.[15]

The state's first line of defense against foreign religion was, thus, again to be the aediles. On their failure the senate entrusted the matter to a senior secular official, the *praetor urbanus*.

But the best known from Livy and most fully treated is the repression of the Bacchanalia in 186 B.C.[16] Dionysian rites were already established at Rome, but Livy relates that the cult came to Etruria via a nameless Greek, and that a Campanian priestess gave the religion at Rome its decisive and destructive turn by admitting men as well as women to the mysteries, by increasing the days of initiation from three per year to five per month, and by holding the initiations at night instead of by day.[17] All sorts of crimes were attributed to the worshippers, who were said to number many thousands. The senate decreed that the investigation of the Bacchanals and their nocturnal rites should be remitted to the consuls, that the priests even in the villages should be sought out so that they could be at the disposal of the consuls, and that edicts restraining the cult should be sent through all Italy.[18] As it happens, the decree as it was sent to the magistrates in the Ager Teuranus in southern Italy has survived, but before we consider it we should look at parts of the speech Livy puts into the mouth of the consul who addressed the people on the senate's decree:

> Never for any gathering, citizens, has this solemn prayer to the gods been not only so apt but also so necessary, a prayer that reminds you that these are the gods whom our forefathers had appointed to be worshipped, to be venerated, to receive our prayers, [3.] not those gods who would drive our minds, as if by the scourges of the Furies, to every crime and every lust with vile and foreign rites.[19]

> For the men wisest in all divine and human law judged nothing was so powerful in destroying religion as where sacrifices were performed not by native but by a foreign ritual.[20]

The close connection between the well-being of the people and the ancient Roman religion is again stressed, as is the danger of the acceptance of foreign rites. And the persons who can best judge of the dangers are those skilled in divine *and human* law. Roman religion is a matter of law.

But the worship of Bacchus was well accepted officially at Rome, hence it could not be abolished, and hence the precise nature of the *senatus consultum*.[21] No one, it declared, is to have a place devoted to the worship of Bacchus. If any persons claim they need such a place they have to appear before the urban praetor at Rome, and the senate is to decide when at least one hundred senators are present. The other provisions are to the same effect: for instance, no Roman or Latin is to associate with the Bacchae, no man is to be a priest, nor shall any man or woman be or appoint a master of the organization, nor shall anyone have a common fund, or take a common oath with them, or vows or stipulations. No one is to hold their rites in secret, nor is there to be more than five persons together to perform such rites, not more than two men and three women. All these provisions are subject to the same qualification that worshippers may be released from them if they appeared before the urban praetor, and the senate consented when more than one hundred senators were present.[22]

All this repression of foreign cults at Rome and among Romans is to be set against their extreme tolerance of foreign religions and rites even among their subject peoples. And at Rome itself foreign worship might be introduced and welcomed if it was at the instigation of the state.[23] The greatest example must be the importation of the Phrygian–Asia Minor goddess, the Magna Mater, from Pergamon in 205 B.C.[24] The background was again the need for victory in the Carthaginian war, and the significance of this is shown by the fact that until a temple was erected to her on the Palatine she was housed in the sanctuary of Victoria.[25] The cult was ecstatic and involved, among other excesses, the self-castration of priests. In the circumstances, despite the acceptance of the goddess it is not surprising that Roman citizens were forbidden active participation in the cult.[26]

A not-too-dissimilar attitude appears with regard to the Druidic religion. Augustus forbade it to Romans but otherwise tolerated it. Claudius abolished it altogether.[27]

Since the main purpose of this chapter is further to elucidate the nature of official Roman religion and its relationship with the state by showing that the response to alien cults is fully consistent with its perceived characteristics, it is not necessary to examine in detail all examples of religious repression. Above all, little now need be said about persecution of Judaism and Christianity when that occurred.[28] Whatever crimes the Roman citizens who were adherents of either religion might be accused of, whether cannibalism or incest or the arson of Rome, repression when it came always included the crime of professing Judaism or Christianity. To confess to being an adherent of Judaism or a Christian was to deny the validity of all other religions, including the Roman state religion, and to refuse to take part in state religious functions. From the standpoint of Roman religion it could not be more obvious that for a citizen to profess Judaism or Christianity was itself a very serious crime.[29]

10 The Pontiffs and Legal Development

The widely held belief that in early society there exists an intimate connection between law and religion takes various forms: that law and religion are at first one and the same; that they are intertwined; or that law emerges from religion. Whatever may be the general accuracy of this thesis, early Roman private law was extremely secular even though its interpretation was in the hands of the pontiffs. The pontiffs were successful aristocratic politicians with no desire, it may be said, to seek the aggrandizement of religion.[1] In previous chapters I have indicated that links between law and religion were rather tenuous. The pontiffs did not take over to law the formalism required for religious acts: they allowed the oath in private law to be paradoxically secular. Yet, despite all this, the two main distinguishing characteristics of Roman private law until at least the late republic are due to its interaction with Roman religion. This is also true of a further, minor, but significant characteristic. There was also an astounding consequence of the role of the pontiffs.

The first of these distinguishing characteristics of Roman legal development was the enormous role of jurists. "Praise of the excellence of Roman law is always of Roman private law. . . . the private law was worked out and elaborated by first the pontiffs, a priestly college, and then the lay jurists," says J. A. C. Thomas.[2] There are two aspects to this issue. First, why was the state or government so willing to entrust legal development to private individuals? The answer is that at first, as we have seen, they were not ordinary private individuals, but the pontiffs, who, in any event, were accustomed to giving legal interpretation. Besides, the pontiffs were patricians, hence they were trusted by the senators and their like to behave properly. Not only that, they had in most cases held top magistracies and proven their reliability to the state system. The opening of the College of Pontiffs to plebeians by the *lex Ogulnia* of 300 B.C. was a defeat for the patricians in more than just the religious sense.[3] Still, the force of tradition and authority was such that patricians dominated the ranks of the jurists until the early first century B.C.[4]

But, as a consequence, the magistrates in charge of operating the court system, the consuls, or the praetors would be very closely bound to the pontiffs interpreting the law. This would remain the case when the pontiffs as interpreters gave way to jurists—they were, after all, the same personalities—and the praetors began to issue edicts and *formulae*. It is, thus, that we can understand the extreme brevity and generality of edict and *formula*—their scope was known and determined by the jurists.[5] In addition, the judges, as senators, with no authority to create law by their decisions, were closely bound to their fellow senators, the praetors and jurists. The legal system was closely knit. Not much would be changed for the system when, in the late republic, senators gave way to *equites* as judge and jurist.

The other aspect of the issue is why were members of the highest caste in society willing to spend their time on legal interpretation? The answer lies in the authority granted to the College of Pontiffs and entrusted by them to one of their number annually to interpret the law. That pontiff's voice was thus the sole true interpretation. Knowledge of law was therefore prestigious. The pontiffs were more willing to accept this task because they were patricians, and lawmaking was to be kept out of the hands of the plebeians. The high prestige attached to giving legal opinions continued even when the College of Pontiffs lost its monopoly of interpretation and when its representative ceased to be authoritative.[6]

Thus, the important role of jurists in legal development arose from the very specific and special place of the College of Pontiffs in Roman public life. The second distinguishing characteristic of Roman law that it owed to religion was the nature of legal reasoning.

It is not always easy for a Western jurist to appreciate the peculiar nature of Roman legal reasoning because, having so influenced subsequent legal reasoning, it is taken as a given. The main fact about Roman legal reasoning is that it is remarkably self-contained. The arguments to a legal decision are legal arguments. In almost all cases a decision is not given on the basis that it is reasonable, just, in accordance with morality or with the dictates of religion, or is socially the most useful. It is, for example, instructive to look at the texts in which the notion of *utilitas*, usefulness, is introduced. In almost all of the cases, *utilitas* is not given as a reason for reaching a decision or framing a rule; rather, at the most, we are told at times that a rule *was* accepted on the ground of utility, *utilitatis causa receptum*.[7] That a decision may be reached or justified on other than "black-letter law" grounds is usually concealed, though sometimes it may be conceded that a rule was created in the past for other reasons. The decision-making process is given the appearance of not being result oriented. Indeed, the reasons given often appear to be preferred as an explanation of the decision, not as arguments for it.

Some examples from the texts will make the point. First, from *D*.30.63 (Celsus, *Digest*, book 17):

> 1. If a testator left a legacy of his slave women and whatever was born from them, and one slave woman died, Servius declared that her offspring was not due because he was legated as an accessory. I consider this to be wrong, and the opinion is in accordance with neither the words nor the intention of the deceased.[8]

We are concerned primarily with the opinion of Servius, which is entirely formalistic and legalistic and seems in no way otherwise to be geared to a satisfactory result. An owner of a female slave or female animal became owner of any offspring: the young were treated as an accessory to the mother. Servius applies this notion of accessory to legacies. A legacy in the form "slave women and their children" is interpreted as meaning that the major bequest is of the women, and children are subsumed within it only as accessories. Hence, if a woman does not pass under the legacy, because she is dead, neither does her child. Servius seems to have no other concern for the interpretation, not even for the intention of the testator.[9] Celsus's own reasoning is also entirely legalistic: interpretation is to depend on the wording and on the intention of the testator.[10]

An example of a similar approach to interpretation by Servius is in *D.* 35.1.40.3 (Javolenus, *Posthumous Works of Labeo*, book 2):

> 2. An owner left a legacy of five *aurei* to his slave, thus: "Let my heir give to my slave Stichus whom I ordered to be free in this will the five *aurei* that I owe him according to my account books." Namusa writes that Servius gave the opinion that there was no legacy given to the slave because an owner could owe nothing to his slave. I think that, following the intention of the owner, a natural rather than a legal debt is to be regarded: and that is the law in force.[11]

Servius's opinion is again very formalistic and legalistic and flouts the clear intention of the testator. Nor does he hold, as he does elsewhere,[12] that where a bequest is specific, a false reason given for it has no effect. Though his reasoning is so formalistic, he may have had a concealed motivation: to insist on the different status of owner and slave and that an owner could never be in debt to the slave.[13] The following is in *D.* 28.7.20pr. (Labeo, *Posthumous Works, Epitomized by Javolenus*, book 2):

3. A woman who owed her husband money which had been promised as dowry, had instituted him as heir on the condition that he neither sued for nor exacted the money promised as dowry. I think that if the husband had notified the other heirs that he was not responsible for a failure to discharge what was due to him as debt, he would at once be heir. But if he were instituted as sole heir with such a condition, I think he will nonetheless at once be heir because an impossible condition is treated as if it were not written.[14]

In this example, there is no real difficulty where the husband is instituted heir along with others. For him to become heir it is enough that he notify the other heirs that he is ready to make *acceptilatio*, that is, give a formal discharge without having received performance. The problem really begins where the husband is appointed sole heir. There is no debtor (standing in place of the wife) to whom he can make *acceptilatio*. Of course, if he were heir, the debt owed on account of the dowry would in any event disappear by the doctrine of *confusio*, since the debtor and creditor would be the same person. But he cannot become heir because he is subject to the condition and there is no one to whom he can fulfill the condition. Still, what the wife had in mind when she appointed her husband as sole heir was that he would become heir unless he had exacted or sued for the debt during her lifetime; but a solution based on the testator's intention was not to be forthcoming. The solution was to declare the condition to be impossible, and an impossible condition was treated as not written.[15] From *G*. 2.244:

4. The question is asked whether we can rightly leave a legacy to a person who is in the power of him whom we institute as heir. Servius thinks one can properly leave such a legacy but the legacy is voided if, at the time when the legacies should vest, he is still in power, and so the legacy is owed whether it was unconditional and he ceased to be in the power of the heir during the lifetime of the testator, or it was conditional and the same happened before the condition was fulfilled. Sabinus and Cassius think the legacy may properly be left under a condition, but not unconditionally: for even if during the lifetime of the testator the legatee ceased to be in the power of the heir, the legacy should be regarded as void because it would be absurd that what would have no effect if the testator died immediately the will was made, would be valid because he lived longer. The authorities of the other school hold the legacy cannot even properly be made under a condition because we can no more be conditional debtors of those in our power than we can be unconditionally.[16]

The background to the dispute is that a son or daughter in *patria potestas*, in the power of father or grandfather, could own nothing. Hence, a legacy left to such a son or daughter actually accrued to the *pater*. What was the result to be if the legatee was in the power of the heir? Servius responds in a very proper legal way: the result depends on the time when the legacy vests. Thus, if the legacy is unconditional, it is valid if the legatee was free from the power of the heir before the testator died. Otherwise the legacy is void. If the legacy is conditional it is valid if at the time the condition is fulfilled (and hence when the legacy should vest) the legatee is no longer in the power of the heir.

The decisions of the later jurists on the issue were affected by the so-called *regula Catoniana*. The rule as such dates only from the early empire, though it derives from an opinion of a republican Cato, and was to the effect that whatever would have been void if the testator had died at the moment he made the will would be void no matter when he died. There were exceptions to the *regula*.[17] On this basis, for Sabinus and Cassius the unconditional legacy that would have been of no effect if the testator had died immediately on making the will is of no effect even if the legatee ceased to be in the power of the heir at the time when the testator actually did die. This decision follows logically once it is accepted that the *regula Catoniana* applies.

But it is precisely here that the otherworldly legalistic approach reveals itself. There is nothing obviously inherently morally wrong or socially objectionable about treating as valid a legacy that would have been unenforceable when the will was made. For instance, if I make a will while I am in the process of purchasing a house but am not yet owner and leave a legacy of it to my wife, and I die after I have become owner, there is no obvious moral or social ground why such a legacy should be void, but it would be under the *regula Catoniana*. It is only the legal fact that there existed a *regula Catoniana* that explains the Sabinian opinion.

The existence of the *regula Catoniana* can itself be explained only on the basis of the self-containment or autonomy of Roman law. We do not know the circumstances in which Cato gave his opinion but we can assume it was based on the making of a will *per aes et libram* (by bronze and scale). This will involved the testator making *mancipatio*, by a variant form, of his property to a person called the *familiae emptor* (taker of the estate). A true *mancipatio* was an actual conveyance, hence Cato was presumably arguing that the only property that could specifically be legated was that owned (and thus capable of conveyance) at the time of the *mancipatio*, that is, when the will was made.[18] This makes fine legal—as distinct from social—sense in its formalism.

But, as often, legal logic is skewed—a fact which serves to highlight its artificiality. First, this approach should, but did not, entail that the only property inherited by the heir was that owned by the testator when he made the will because only that would have been conveyed by the *mancipatio*. Second, the testator's whole property should have been conveyed by the *mancipatio* to the *familiae emptor*, who should have been under an obligation to transfer it to the heir.[19] But it seems that the *familiae emptor* acquired nothing, the property was not conveyed away from the testator, and the heir became owner, without any conveyance to him, when he accepted the inheritance. In these circumstances there was no need to develop the *regula Catoniana* at all, far less use it as here to oust the clear intention of the testator. What is most striking is that it was developed and used here in early classical law, after the time of Servius, who gave the most appropriate decision.

But Sabinus and Cassius treat the conditional legacy as valid and effective if the condition is realized after the legatee is free from the *potestas* of the heir. The Proculians, on the other hand, regard even a conditional legacy as void on the express ground that one could no more be a conditional debtor to someone in one's power than be an unconditional debtor.[20] This is even more remote from the testator's intention. If, as I tend to think, this Proculian view is more in accordance with legal logic, then it is instructive that the Sabinians who moved from it still held to the invalidity of the unconditional legacy. The following is from *D.* 1.5.14 (Paul, *Views*, book 4):

5. Those who are procreated abnormally, in a shape different from that of human form, do not count as children: for instance, if a woman gave birth to some kind of monster or prodigy. But an offspring that has more limbs than are used by man seems to be fully formed, and therefore is counted among children.[21]

This is the text as it appears in Justinian's *Digest* under the title "On human status" in a very nonspecific context. Paul's ruling seems to be of general application and relates to any legal situation that involves an abnormal birth. Then the distinction seems arbitrary (except on the basis of abstract legal reasoning): a child born of monstrous shape does not count as an offspring for any legal purpose; a child born with more than the usual number of limbs is fully formed and therefore, legally, in Paul's opinion, does count as an offspring. The distinction, whether the child lives or dies, whether the legal issue concerns benefits to child or parents, makes no moral, medical, or social sense. It can be justified only, if at all, on the basis of the formal reasoning that an offspring that is fully formed counts as a child, hence that status is retained by one who is more than fully formed. An offspring that, in contrast, does not have the normal human shape is not a child. Justinian's law, here as elsewhere, retains the old mode of pontifical, goalless, legal reasoning.

But in this instance we have more information on the jurist's views. The text derives from Paul's *Sententiae* (4.9.3), which have come down to us, and there we have a fuller version:

> A woman, if she gave birth to some kind of monster or prodigy, achieves nothing: for they do not count as children that are procreated abnormally in a shape different from that of human form. [4.] It is settled that an offspring who doubles the use of human limbs, because on this account he seems to have achieved something, does advantage the mother.[22]

The context of this, for Paul, was the *senatus consultum Tertullianum* of Hadrian's time (117–138 A.D.), which decreed that a female Roman citizen who had the *ius liberorum* (right of children, achieved on the birth of a fixed number of children) could, on intestacy, inherit from a deceased child. Her claim in that event was not the first but was postponed to that of persons in the power (*potestas*) of the child who became free of *potestas* on his death, next to that of the father, finally to that of brothers (of the child) on the father's side. When the mother did succeed, she shared the estate with sisters on the father's side. In the situation of a monstrous birth, the only realistic case of inheritance by the mother would be where the offspring inherited from his or her father, who had died almost at the time of the child's birth, and the mother, if freeborn, already had two children, or three if she were a freed woman. Not only would the case be excessively rare but the *consultum Tertullianum*, of which we do not have the wording, is most unlikely to have defined "child."[23] As in Justinian's *Digest*, so in the specific context of the *senatus consultum Trebellianum:* Paul's distinction cannot be result oriented but derives from the form of reasoning inherited from the pontiffs.[24]

There is no need to multiply these examples.[25] The reasoning in them is typical of Roman law (though they were chosen to exemplify that reasoning in situations in which it would be outlandish or striking in some way). What has to be stressed is that the reasoning is self-contained. The arguments to, or explanation of, a legal opinion or rule are based on lawness, not justice, efficiency, utility, or other social values. The reasoning is that which we have already seen in chapter 1 for sacred law in dealing with such questions as May one chapel be made sacred to two deities? or May a vow of an uncertain amount of money be made to a deity?

The form of reasoning is completely appropriate for Roman sacred law. In determining how humans were to keep in proper contact with the gods, it was out of the question in the Roman context to base a ruling on what would be just or efficient or useful to the state. Only the rules of religious law could give the answer. But reliance on nonlegal values is often appropriate in developing rules of private law, and the relative infrequency of such reliance in the Roman legal sources can be explained only on the basis that accepted modes of interpretation of private law grew up in the hands of the pontiffs, who simply approached the issues in private law in the way they approached the issues of sacred law. These modes of interpretation, once established, continued even when interpretation was no longer the monopoly of the pontiffs, and even when it was no longer the preserve of the senators. This is to be expected in a discipline as traditional as law. Juristic reasoning in the empire proceeds in the same way as in the republic.[26]

Moreover, probably also from pontifical reasoning comes another feature of legal argumentation. As we also saw in chapter 1, a pontifical opinion might be respected because of the authority of the respondent. The same is true of juristic opinions. Thus, Cicero writes playfully to his friend, the jurist Trebatius, who was campaigning with Caesar: "I very much fear you will freeze during the winter. Therefore I think (and the same was the decision of Mucius and Manilius) that you should make use of a blazing fire, especially since you have no abundance of cloaks."[27] Cicero's humor lies in citing other jurists in support of his recommendation, and can be fun only if such citation was commonplace among the jurists. But it is then noteworthy that here—and in many legal texts—the argumentation of the cited jurists is not given. To support the proposition, the similar opinion of distinguished jurists was authority enough.

The minor characteristic that Roman law owes to the involvement of the pontiffs is that law was built up for individual situations without any examination of the true state of the facts. It was stressed in chapter 1 that when the pontiffs gave a judgment they usually did so without examining the facts.[28] Likewise, the jurists in the later republic would give an opinion on the law when consulted by a private individual and when they could have heard only one version of the facts. Cicero records:

> I, indeed, have often heard my father and my father-in-law say that our people who wanted to win high honor for knowledge would embrace all subjects which were then known in the country. They remembered Sextus Aelius. We have actually seen Manius Manilius walking across the forum, and what is remarkable is that in so doing he was putting his store of advice to the use of all citizens. People resorted to them both walking and sitting in their seat at home, not only to consult them about the civil law, but also about marrying a daughter, buying a farm, cultivating a field, in short about every duty or business.[29]

The Pontiffs and Legal Development

> For it is beyond doubt that the house of a jurisconsult is the oracle of the whole state. Evidence of this is the gateway and forecourt of our friend Quintus Mucius, which are daily thronged by a great crowd of citizens, including persons of the highest distinction, even despite his very poor health and great age.[30]

In the circumstances described, these jurists were not giving a judgment after due consideration of all the facts. They were stating their opinion of the state of the law as it applied to the facts proposed to them.[31]

Likewise in the empire, it was common for individuals to present petitions (*libelli*) to the emperor, setting out their statement of the facts and asking for a ruling on the law. The petitions would be forwarded to the appropriate department (*a libellis*), which would set out the response, the emperor would add *scripsi* ("I have written") or *subscripsi*, and the petitioner could obtain a certified copy. Again, there is no examination of the accuracy of the facts and no judgment here. But if the response were favorable to the petitioner's claim it would be useful to him. In any subsequent lawsuit, for example, if he could establish that the facts were as he stated them in the petition, then he could use the *subscriptio* as proof of the law.[32]

One direct consequence of the promulgation of the Twelve Tables and, especially, of giving their interpretation to the pontiffs was truly stupendous. Custom was denied almost any further role in the development of Roman law.[33] The full significance of this is easily overlooked, partly because we are concerned with a negative—custom had no role in Roman law—partly because modern Western law is custom-free. But until recent times, apart from the Reception of Roman law, the main factor in the growth of Western law was custom: witness the numerous *coutumes* of the regions of France and Belgium, the *fueros* of Spain, the *forais* of Portugal, and the *Weistümer* of medieval Germany.[34] In England, the customs that made law were the customs of the judges.[35] But at Rome, judge-made law was also necessarily excluded: interpretation was the preserve of the pontiffs (and their successors, the jurists).

But if there is one feature that should be special to customary law it is that it should emerge from the people and be to a considerable extent the reflection of society.[36] In contrast, development by an official, organized body such as the College of Pontiffs, which has its own style of reasoning—reasoning that is artificial in the field of private law—makes for a law that is as autonomous as possible. It is this that accounts for the apparent timelessness of law in the last century of the republic and in the principate. No other system of law in the Western world can be studied and described historically with so little reference to the surrounding social, economic, and political conditions.[37]

But one must go further still. Custom and judicial decisions were, of necessity, denied a role in lawmaking. But the Twelve Tables, no matter how extensively interpreted, could not form a whole modern legal system. Unless successive Roman "governments" were to show an interest in legislating private law that would be quite unusual—and they did not[38]—then some other official source of making law would have to be created. That source was to be the Edict of the praetor. In this way too, handing the interpretation of the Twelve Tables over to the pontiffs was to lead to a development of law that was different from anywhere else in the world.

11 The Paradox Resolved

A central, if mostly unstated, issue of this book has been a paradox or apparent paradox; the Romans of the republic were known for their adherence to religious observance, yet they produced a system of law that is remarkable for its secularity even though legal development was long in the hands of the College of Pontiffs. We are now in a position to address this issue directly.

The promulgation of the Twelve Tables was decisive for the development of Roman private law and the state. This code of around 450 B.C. was the product of a struggle between the patricians and the plebeians in which the main demand of the latter was legislation, preferably issued by themselves, setting out and restricting the powers of the higher magistrates and giving equality of treatment among citizens. Tired by the years of struggle, the plebeians finally agreed that the patricians could form the legislation. The result was the Twelve Tables. The Twelve Tables is very much a code prepared by patricians for plebeians. Everything is omitted that the former considered was no concern of the latter. Hence, there is a total absence of public law in the sense of the law relating to public officials. The plebeians lost this important battle. Livy is wide of the mark when he claims that the Twelve Tables were the fountainhead of both public and private law.[1] Hence, too, the complete omission of anything touching on the state religion. That was the business of the four main colleges of priests, especially of the College of Pontiffs, and the priests (until considerably later) all had to be patricians.

The Twelve Tables present a very misleading picture of the law as a whole, and of how people behaved in practice. As a code of law, they do, of course, show law as it was. But the picture they provide is very partial in two major respects. First, they present the law as very egalitarian. In fact, probably more than other ancient societies, Rome was marked by important legal differences between one group and the next. Second, they present the law as devoid of religious input. In practice, legal acts would be marked by religious observances.

Scholars often stress that the Twelve Tables are a code of law for peasants.[2] It would perhaps be more illuminating to emphasize that they are very egalitarian; indeed one might say that the Twelve Tables are geared to the lowest common denominator of society. With three or perhaps four exceptions, each provision of the code applies to the whole range of society. We have already considered three legal acts concerning family relations that obviously were, at least in practice, restricted to the uppermost ranks of society: the creation of *manus* by *confarreatio*, *adrogatio*, and the making of a will *calatis comitiis*. Of these, only *confarreatio* may have been mentioned in the Twelve Tables and, if it was, it was done so incidentally in connection with *usus*. The general view probably is that there was no such provision.

If we leave aside any possible provision on *confarreatio*, then only three clauses relate to a difference in treatment according to rank in society. Each is revealing in its own way for the nature of the codification.

The first is the notorious provision that forbade intermarriage between patrician and plebeian. This is the only known provision dealing with capacity for, or requirements of, marriage. There is nothing on age requirements, nationality, personal status, the necessary consents, or the forbidden degrees of relationship. The provision is represented in the sources as an innovation, as the work of the second set of *decemviri*, who had turned tyrannous.[3] Since there are no other provisions on capacity, the account of the sources seems plausible. Indeed, this is the best evidence that exists in the clauses of the code for the claim that the second *decemviri* were tyrannous. The provision would lend support to an opinion that the patricians, having won the battle to be the legislators, first issued ten tables of law that were remarkably egalitarian, then, with renewed confidence and arrogance after the good reception of that code, again humiliated the plebeians.[4]

It can scarcely be too strongly emphasized how astonishing it is that this is the only provision of the code that even seems to mention, far less make a distinction between, patrician and plebeian. Yet, the second provision that concerns a distinction between groups may in part at least concern the division between patrician and plebeian, but it is to a very different effect. According to Roman tradition, whose accuracy we need not here discuss, Romulus entrusted the plebeians to the care of the patricians, and each plebeian was entitled to choose a patron for himself. Thus was the law of patronage established.[5] Reciprocal (but different) legal rights and duties were then assigned to patron and client, and a breach of a duty was to be regarded as treason, and punishable by death.[6] The equivalent provision of the Twelve Tables states: "If a patron commits a wrong on his client, let the patron be *sacer*."[7] The provision is unilateral: it is the patron who is to abstain from harming his client.

It would appear that by this time any specific legal rights and duties between patron and client had disappeared.[8] But, nonetheless, the supreme sanction is to be inflicted on a patron who injures a client. The only provision in the Twelve Tables on patronage is, thus, one beneficial to the underclass.

The last provision that reveals a legal division between groups is very different: "For a landowner [*assiduus*], let the protector [*vindex*] be a landowner. For a proletarian [*proletarius*], let anyone who is willing be protector."[9] In an early *actio in personam* a defendant summoned before the magistrate had to go and could not release himself from the power of the plaintiff that was authorized against him. But a third party, *vindex*, could intervene to relieve him.[10] The nature of the *vindex*, who appears to act as guarantor or cautioner, is unclear, but it seems that he himself became liable to the plaintiff. The point of the provision is, therefore, that for a wealthy person or landowner, *assiduus*, only a wealthy person could act as guarantor, whereas anyone could so act for a person ranked as a *proletarius*. That is, the property qualification demanded from a *vindex* depended not at all on the amount of the suit, but on the rank of the defendant for whom he was acting.

The precise meaning of *assiduus* and *proletarius* is not easily determined, though the latter would seem to be the poorest citizens not included in the 193 centuries of the Servian constitution, and who were not even normally allowed to serve in the army.[11] If *assidui* and *proletarii* are terms that exhaust all the categories of citizens, then an *assiduus* would be any citizen wealthy enough to be included in one of the centuries. The precise distinction need not detain us. What matters is that in this provision of the Twelve Tables that made a distinction between groups of citizens a concession was being made to the poorest. When placed with the other provisions (before the second *decemviri*) the egalitarian nature of the codification is revealed.

But when we turn away from the Twelve Tables and private law to other parts of law, legal divisions between one group and another are striking. It is not just that patricians are treated differently from plebeians, but that, as we shall see, the political legal rights of one group of citizens differ from those of another group. I stress "political *legal* rights." One would expect that in practice the political rights of rich and poor would differ with a marked bias in favor of the former. What is more remarkable is that differences between patricians and plebeians (not always the same thing as rich and poor) in political rights are enshrined in law. To choose examples:

1. Only patricians could be pontiffs or augurs until the *lex Ogulnia* of 300 B.C.[12] As a result of the efforts of the tribunes Licinius and Sextius from 377 B.C., the so-called *leges Liciniae Sextiae* were passed in 367.[13] Among other things they provided that the keepers of the oracles and the Sybilline books, now increased to ten—the *decemviri sacris faciundis*—had to be five patricians and five plebeians.[14] This was a big advance for the plebeians, since the reading of the oracles could have significant political consequences.

2. Only patricians could be consuls until the *leges Liciniae Sextiae*. Thereafter, one had to be a plebeian, but this seems not to have been regularly observed until 320 B.C. The consuls were the normal heads of state. From 444 B.C., however, instead of consuls the chief magistracy could be, and frequently was for a considerable period, a college of three military tribunes, and plebeians could hold that office. But, according to Livy, plebeians were not elected until 400 B.C.[15] Dictators who were appointed in an emergency had to be patricians.

The only other regular magistrates in the early republic were the quaestors, who were appointed by the consuls as their assistants. Plebeians became eligible in 421.

In 367, the year of the first plebeian consul, the office of praetor was created—at first only one was elected per year—specifically to deal with legal matters. According to Livy, the office was confined to patricians, but this has been doubted because there was a plebeian praetor—the first, says Livy—in 337, and there is no trace of any intervening legislation.[16]

3. Of the assemblies, much has been said of the *comitia curiata*, but this had not the political power in historical times that it may once have had. The most important assembly was the *comitia centuriata* for which the people were, according to the historians, divided on a military basis into five classes, each consisting of centuries, membership in a class being dependent on wealth. The first, wealthiest, class had eighty centuries; the second, third, and fourth had twenty each; and the fifth class had thirty. All of these were infantry. Attached to the first class were two centuries of engineers, and to the fifth class, two centuries of buglers and trumpeters. Above the first class and presumably drawn from its wealthier members were eighteen centuries of calvary, the *equites*. At the bottom were the *proletarii*, those who did not have the minimum requirement for the fifth class, and they formed one century and were excused from military service.[17]

This is the construction of the *comitia centuriata* attributed to the sixth king, Servius, in the sixth century B.C. There is general agreement that the overall picture is accurately drawn, though there is doubt about details.[18]

The *comitia centuriata* was the main legislative body. It could meet only when summoned by the consuls, it could not deal with business other than that put before it by these magistrates, it could not amend any proposed legislation, though it could vote it down. For voting in the *comitia centuriata*, Livy (having discussed the financial and military burdens which were heaviest on the higher classes) reports:

> All these burdens were shifted from the poor to the rich. [10.] Privileges were then granted to the latter. For suffrage by man to man was not given (as it was said to be by Romulus and retained by the other kings) promiscuously to all with the same force and with the same right, but gradations were introduced so that neither should anyone seem to be excluded from suffrage yet all the power should be with the leaders of the state. [11.] For the *equites* were called upon to vote first. Then the eighty centuries of the first class. Then if there was any difference in opinion, which rarely happened, it was provided that the second class be called, and it almost never happened that it descended so low as to reach the lowest citizens.[19]

Thus, the classes were called in order by centuries. Since there were 193 centuries altogether, of which the *equites* had 18 and the first class 80, if the *equites* and first class voted in the same way, they had an absolute majority and the vote would not be taken further. Since, in any event, the classes were by no means composed of equal numbers of citizens, it will be appreciated that by law the political rights of, say, the fifth class and the *proletarii* on the one hand, and of the first class on the other, were very different.[20] Further elaboration is not necessary, except that it should be noted that the magistrates with *imperium* and (subsequently) the censors were elected by the *comitia centuriata*.[21]

4. The most striking difference enshrined in law between different groups of citizens relates to who could be appointed a judge. There was a list of who could be chosen to act as judge whether in civil or criminal cases, and until the *lex iudiciaria* of C. Sempronius Gracchus in 122 B.C., only senators could be on the list. This statute admitted *equites equo publico* (knights provided with a horse at public expense) to the list and apparently excluded senators.[22] As Claude Nicolet says, "By a striking dichotomy, even civil suits between Romans were to be judged by men who were not only the richest in the community but were organized in an *ordo*, a regular constitutional body whose membership and activities were closely supervised by the state."[23] (An important deduction should be made from the social rank of the judges, even though it cannot strictly be proved from the written sources. Senatorial judges, conscious of their status, are unlikely to pay too much attention to the opinions of nonsenatorial jurists. Equestrian judges will tend also to pay attention to jurists who are *equites*, but

not to those of lesser status. This would be a factor in keeping jurisprudence an aristocratic science and helps to explain the well-known fact that until the end of the second century B.C. the leading jurists were all of senatorial rank, while the knights came to the fore in the first century B.C.).[24]

In view of the foregoing one might be tempted to advance the claim that Roman private law was precisely that area of law where the patricians were willing to be placed on a footing of equality with plebeians. That would, at any rate, adequately describe the contents of the Twelve Tables.[25]

The second regard in which the Twelve Tables, because of the background to their promulgation, present a very misleading picture is in the absence of religion from the provisions. Sacred law and all aspects of state religion are omitted. These were the business of the four main colleges of priests, especially of the College of Pontiffs, and the priests all had to be patricians. Sacred law and the state religion were not appropriate subjects for the plebeians.

But early Roman religion below the highest "official" level was basically a peasant religion. That peasant religion was not acknowledged in the law, perhaps because the patrician legislators were too little interested: the absence of a moral content in Roman religion meant that it could not be used directly as a tool for instruction.[26]

Thus, the law in the Twelve Tables, and Roman private law in general, is quite remarkably secular in appearance. And so it was, in one sense, in reality. With a few exceptions, which we have already seen, such as *confarreatio* and *iusiurandum liberti*, the performance of religious acts had no consequences for the validity or invalidity of legal acts. In another sense, in daily life, law and religion were not kept separate. In practice, religious observances were a constant aspect of Roman life. But they were not used to validate legal acts. A few examples will make this clearer.

Thus, for the legal contracting of a marriage (except for *confarreatio*), whether with or without *manus*, no religious act was necessary, or efficacious. But religious acts were standard. For instance, a woman who had not previously been married laid aside her girl's clothing, *toga praetexta*, on the day before the wedding and dedicated it, with her toys, to the gods, originally to the household gods of her father's house.[27] In early times, before the first century B.C., the marriage celebration began with taking private auspices, and would include the sacrifice of an animal which could be examined by *haruspices*.[28] Cicero relates that even in his day nuptial auspices were regularly taken, though they had lost their religious significance.[29] After the bride had been led to her husband's home (*deductio in domum*) she prayed by the marriage bed (which had been placed in the future living room) to the gods of her new home for a happy marriage.[30] On the following day, at the feast called *repotia*, she brought her first sacrifice to the household gods.

We can choose another example from the very different field of contract. We have already seen that, apart from the anomalous case of *iusiurandum liberti*, the taking of an oath had no legal force. But it should be observed that in practice an oath would commonly be used in private-law contexts, but the oath as such produced no legal effects. Thus, Cato, in *De agri cultura* (146), sets out the terms for making contracts for milling olives. One term was that each worker was to take an oath that neither he nor anyone with his connivance had stolen olives or oil. If anyone failed to take the oath, his share of pay was not due. The legal force of this depends entirely on the requirement to take the oath being a term of the contract, and the force would be exactly the same if the requirement had been not to take an oath but to make a declaration that he had not stolen. The divine was everywhere, only not in private law.

Interpretation of the Twelve Tables was handed over to the College of Pontiffs, who selected one of its members each year for the task. It was this fact that was to give developing Roman law its major characteristics. Law was to be not religious but pontifical. First, because of this, the state accepted lawmaking, interpretation, by private individuals—pontiffs and patricians in the first place; and private individuals of the highest rank were willing to give time to develop law. The famous central role of jurists in developing Roman private law thus resulted from the interpretation of the Twelve Tables being entrusted to the College of Pontiffs. Even at the beginning of the first century B.C., the *pontifex maximus* Quintus Mucius, in his great commentary *Ius Civile*, retains civil law in its technical or semitechnical sense as "the interpretation of the Twelve Tables." Second, juristic reasoning for private law is recognizably pontifical reasoning for sacred law. The arguments may not be given or they may rely on authority, but otherwise they are internal legal arguments based on the nature of the situations. There are no juristic appeals to the good of the state, public or private utility, best economic outcome, justice, or morality. Such appeals obviously have no place in determining how men should conduct themselves to be in the right relationship with the deities. But their irrelevance is not obvious for deciding issues of private law. This style of reasoning not only remained characteristic, but without it Roman law could not subsequently have been so easily borrowed.

Yet the pontiffs and, after them, the jurists do not carry over to private law the attributes of religion, as is often believed. The excessive attention paid to form for the validity of religious acts such as vows and prayers is not carried over to private law, except for the one case of the contract of *stipulatio*, a fact that may confirm that the contract had its origins in religion. Even in the few instances where an oath was given legal effect, the oath was used for purely secular ends and, indeed, was employed because of a specific lack in the secular system. Indeed, in the *iusiurandum in litem*, the oath sworn as to the value of his lawsuit by the plaintiff, it was accepted by the jurists—at some stage—that he would overstate his claim.

A similar lack of interest in the preservation of private religious values is shown when, as we shall now see, Publius Mucius devised a dodge whereby a legatee could take the legacy without being liable to take over the religious obligations of the deceased.

The *sacra* of individual families were also, though in a rather different way, within the care of the pontiffs. Persons who succeeded to property on someone's death were, in a fixed order, bound to perform the *sacra* of the deceased. Somewhere between the mid-third and late second century B.C. an old order of obligation was replaced by the following order:[31] first, the heir (or heirs); second, whoever by a *donatio mortis causa* or by will took as much as all the heirs together; third, in the absence of an heir, whoever by usucaption acquired the greatest part of the deceased's property; fourth, if no one took any of the deceased's property, the creditor who retained the most; fifth (and last), any debtor of the deceased who did not pay.[32]

Performance of the *sacra* was burdensome, and at least as early as the playwright Plautus, to receive an inheritance while avoiding the *sacra* was regarded as a special pleasure.[33] And Festus tells us that *sine sacris hereditas* was proverbial for obtaining an advantage without inconvenience.[34]

In this context, Publius Mucius Scaevola, consul in 133 B.C. and *pontifex maximus*,[35] was responsible for at least one dodge that enabled a legatee who was left as much as the heirs to avoid responsibility for the *sacra*. He advised that the legatee simply accept less than the full amount of the legacy so that he did take less than the heirs.[36]

Cicero scoffs at Publius and Quintus Mucius, *pontifices maximi*, for their pretension that one could not be a good pontiff without a knowledge of the civil law.[37] And he points out that by the device just discussed, the Scaevolae used a knowledge of the civil law to negate the rules of the pontiffs.[38] The criticism seems justified. We have here for private religious cults an example of the manipulation that, used in state religious observances, gave rise to cynicism among educated Romans. Publius's dodge suggests that for him it was immaterial for the welfare of the deceased, his family, or the state that the private *sacra* were observed.

(On a very different level and incidentally, it may be observed that the reason-

The Paradox Resolved

ing behind the dodge was very pontifical and formal and similar to the one we observed in the interpretation in the case of the Capitoline head. The deceased left the legatee as much as he left the heir.[39] The rule of obligation for the *sacra* was formulated [by the Mucii?] in terms not of entitlement but of taking; hence the legatee by taking less could determine his own fate. Other factors, such as the testator's wishes and benefits to society, are excluded).

Instructive also is the approach to the calendar, which was again the concern of the pontiffs. The types of days were distinguished in various ways, but some were marked with *F* for *fas*, some others with *N* for *nefas*, yet others with a *C* for *comitialis*, or with one of two other designations (which need not concern us). The praetor (originally, the consul) could not without sin take part in a *legis actio* on an *N* day.[40] Thus, the value of the Twelve Tables as setting out the law was limited for the plebeians unless they also knew on which days a *legis actio* could be brought. But the calendar was not published and was a secret of the pontiffs until its publication, traditionally by Cn. Flavius, who was curule aedile in 304 A.D. We should see in this another defeat of the plebeians in 451 B.C. In this context it must be significant that very much later Varro wrote that if a praetor did conduct a *legis actio* inadvertently on a *dies nefastus* he could be released from his sin by a sacrifice but that if he acted knowingly Quintus Mucius said his sin could not be expiated.[41] This text indicates that even someone so high in the Roman hierarchy as a praetor, who did not have his calendar with him might unintentionally hold court on a *dies nefastus*.[42] The difficulty that plebeians would have in bringing an action when they had no access to the calendar can be readily imagined.

It is, of course, entirely reasonable that the consuls (and then the praetors), who had many other duties, should have numerous days set aside in each year in which they did not have to hear lawsuits. But it was the pontiffs who had control of the calendar and decided which days were which. Since the will of the gods was not made manifest in a revealed religious code, we have to say that it was the authority of the pontiffs that closed certain days to magistrates involving themselves with a *legis actio*.[43]

At first sight it may appear strange that it was *sinful* for a magistrate to hear a *legis actio* on a prohibited day, even though the intention was to free the magistrate for other business. But reflection will show there was no other choice. The pontiffs were religious officers with no powers of coercion. If they wished to prohibit conduct—and it was needful for the pontiffs here to do so—they could only declare it sinful. And since the calendar was not published it would have been pointless and tactless to place the sin on the petitioner for the action. Presumably it was because the behavior of the magistrate was either religiously proper or was sinful that the days were designated as being *fas* or *nefas*. But one point needs to be stressed. *Dies fasti* and *dies nefasti* are not otherwise significant for religious or secular activity. There are no religious observances that are appropriate on one or the other type of day. There is no other work that is inhibited on *dies nefasti*, except that also prohibited were the acts particular to *dies comitiales*, when comitia might be summoned, or when verdicts might be given in some kinds of criminal cases.[44] It is plausible to suggest that here we have an early example of the manipulation of religion for state purposes: it was convenient for the patricians if the days were limited in which the people could assemble.[45]

The Roman texts, though, that define or appear to define *dies nefasti* are all concerned with the activity of the praetor. The main point of the distinction between *dies fasti* and *dies nefasti* appears to be whether the praetor might or might not properly conduct a *legis actio*.[46]

A consequence, therefore, that may perhaps be fairly regarded as largely accidental is that the consul or praetor's conduct in hearing a *legis actio* was given a religious coloring. The pontiffs set the calendar. Necessity required that certain days be closed to *legis actiones*. The sole option available to the pontiffs was to declare sinful the conduct of a magistrate hearing a *legis actio* on such a day. From the necessary involvement of the pontiffs a religious element is introduced into the conduct of magistrates that otherwise need have no place and that otherwise has no significance.

The detail points up the very close connection between the official state religion and governmental or state action. But it might also suggest that some (or much) of Roman state religious activity was not religion in the sense in which we use the term. It makes easier the claim that the fact of the pontifical monopoly of legal interpretation is, in itself, no indication of a religious content to law. It even helps to explain such things as the very restricted role of the oath in Roman private law, and the extreme secularity of this oath.

Indeed, when discussing the role of the oath in Roman private law I suggested it was an example of what I wanted to call the "second best" in law. The designation of days on which the consul or praetor might not hear *legis actiones* as *nefasti* also approaches this notion of the "second best." The dilemma was that many days had to be kept free from the task of hearing *legis actiones*, since the consul had other important functions. The pontiffs had the task of regulating the calendar, so to them fell the obligation of finding a basis to explain why on many days *legis actiones* could not be heard. This approach differs from classic instances of the "second best" only in that, once it was accepted that the dilemma had to be resolved and by them, they had no alternative approach: they had to declare it *nefas* for the consul to hear *legis actiones*. They had no other sanction or legal weapon in their armory.

Almost as an appendix to this chapter, and also to bolster the conclusions, something must be said about a few individuals who were important in the development of early Roman law. Various texts tell of Cn. Flavius who was curule aedile in 304 B.C.

> In one of them you request an account of Gnaeus Flavius, son of Annius. He did not live before the *decemviri* because he was a curule aedile, and that office was created many years after the *decemviri*. "What therefore did he achieve by publishing the calendar?" It is thought that at one time the list was kept secret so that a day for bringing a *legis actio* would be sought by few people. There is much authority that Gnaeus Flavius, the secretary, published the calendar and composed a list of the forms of action, so you need not think that I or rather Africanus (for he is talking) made this up.[47]

> In any event, there is scarcely any disagreement about the stubbornness of his [Gnaeus Flavius's] struggle with the nobles who despised his low birth. [5.] He published the civil law hidden in the archives of the pontiffs and posted up the calendar on white notice boards around the forum, so that people might know when they could bring a *legis actio*.[48]

> Thereafter when Appius Claudius had composed and set out in standard form the *legis actiones*, his clerk Gnaeus Flavius, the son of a freedman, stole the book and delivered it to the people. This service was so pleasing to the people that he became a tribune of the plebs, a senator and curule aedile.[49]

The texts are not consistent in detail. But if in general they are accurate, Gnaeus Flavius published both the calendar and the forms of *legis actiones*; neither of these was generally known before; and it is significant that his act was very pleasing to the populace.[50]

Tiberius Coruncanius was the first plebeian *pontifex maximus* and was consul in 280 B.C. Of him Pomponius reports:

> Very many and very great men have professed knowledge of the civil law. But those who were held in the highest honor by the Roman people are those of whom an account must be given in the present book so that it may appear by whom, by what quality of men, this law arose and was handed down. Of all those who mastered this science, tradition records that no one before Tiberius Coruncanius made public profession of it. The others up to this time either thought it right to keep the law hidden and only gave private consultations, rather than offered themselves to people who wanted to learn the law.[51]

The text is not free from ambiguity.[52] It need not be taken as meaning that pontiffs before Coruncanius had never given *responsa* in public.[53] It does indicate that, according to tradition, Coruncanius was the first to give some kind of organized instruction in law, and that previously in some sense law was treated as a private, concealed science by those who knew it. We have no way of establishing whether or not Coruncanius was the first to give instruction in law. If he was, then it is significant that he was the first plebeian *pontifex maximus*. The opening up of the College of Pontiffs to plebeians by the *lex Ogulnia* in 300 B.C. was at the same time an opening up of the civil law to the plebeians. Once again we see how little the promulgation of the Twelve Tables was a victory for the plebeians.[54]

Sextus and Publius Aelius Paetus are the earliest known jurists who were not pontiffs, though Publius was an augur. Sextus was consul in 198 B.C. and wrote one of the earliest known Roman law books. Of it Pomponius writes: "Ennius, indeed, praised Sextus Aelius, and there exists a book of his that is entitled *Tripertita* ['The three parts'], which book contains, as it were, the cradle of the law. It is called *Tripertita* because the clause of the Twelve Tables is set out, to it is joined the interpretation, and under that is given the *legis actio*."[55] Thus, one of the two earliest known nonpontifical jurists was active in promulgating knowledge of the Twelve Tables, which was once the secret presence of the College of Pontiffs. Of course, if the accounts of the activities of Coruncanius, Gnaeus Flavius, and Sextus Aelius are not historically accurate, then it is almost as significant that Roman tradition recorded the opening up of the knowledge of the law as part of the struggle between the patricians and plebeians, and it was a great boon to the latter.

In conclusion we should return to the claim of the Scaevolae that no one could be a good pontiff without knowledge of the civil law. Cicero mocks: "Of all of it? Why so? For of what use to the pontiff is the law of party walls or of water rights or, in fact, of any of it, except that which is connected with religion?"[56] True, except that the Scaevolae may not have been talking of substantive law but of legal techniques, and then they would have been correct. Private-law reasoning derived from pontifical reasoning, but such was the development of private law that private-law approaches became important to religious decisions. Roman private law owes its special characteristics to its early dependence on the pontiffs, the nature of Roman religion, and the intimate relationship between Roman religion and the state.

Roman religion concerned the right relations between people and the deities. It had no theology. It did not prescribe conduct. There was emphasis on formalities and observances which could affect outcomes. Roman private law concerned the right relations between man and man and, of course, did prescribe conduct. The absence of theology from Roman religion which controlled legal development resulted in law that was remarkably secular. There was nothing like the same need in private law for formalities, and the requirements there were looser. There was not the same need for the words pronounced in a lawsuit (by *legis actio*) to be flawless, as for the words in a prayer. Even in the few cases where religious forms were used in private law, as with oaths, they appear as a type of "the second best," devoid of a religious or supernatural content. Roman private law illuminates the lack of spirituality in Roman religion. Indeed, the very "lawness" of early Roman law that was noted at the end of chapter 2 is itself a result of the nature of Roman religion.

I should like to restate the principal conclusions in a rather different way. Roman society was very hierarchical. Roman religion was "hierarchized." Only patricians could be pontiffs until 300 B.C. Roman religion was very much the concern of the government. Its main business was to preserve the right relationship between the Roman gods on the one hand, and the Roman state, its leading officials, and its armies on the other. Only an assembly of the state or a properly appointed magistrate with the appropriate authority could consecrate property to a god. Not even pontiffs could. Roman religion was very closely connected with state policy and could be manipulated to that end without impropriety. The state religion did not give rise to an ethical system of behavior.

Roman law was also much "hierarchized." Pressure from the plebeians led the patricians to promulgate the Twelve Tables, but very much *de haut en bas*. The plebeians wanted equality of law, and this was granted by the Twelve Tables, but not for the subject matter that the plebs wanted. The Twelve Tables, taken in isolation from the rest of law, are very egalitarian: they contain only that part of the law that the patricians were willing to share with the plebeians. They also concern the relations of one private individual with another, not with the state. Hence, there was no real place for state religion in the codification, and it was in any event inappropriate because that was the preserve of the pontiffs. The *ius civile* developed from the interpretation of the Twelve Tables by the pontiffs.

The pontiffs built up the law on the basis of the principles of interpretation that they used for religious law. This presumably would be unconscious. But they did not introduce into law the strict formalism that was demanded for religious rites. That formalism was the content of the state religion and determined relations with the gods. But strict formalism was not needed and was inappropriate for relations between one individual and another. An exception to this was the *stipulatio* that, probably, had ancient religious roots. When, as occurred only very occasionally, a religious element in the form of an oath was introduced into private law, it was for purely secular ends, to circumvent a secular problem. Religious aspects of such an oath were not treated seriously.

Of course, there was much Roman "folk" religion below the "state" religion, but this was not allowed to have an impact on legal rules or institutions. Religion was a different science from law. We have here a fine example of an intellectual tendency, noticeable in Roman private law, of seeing a subject as consisting of self-contained and self-referential blocks: legal procedure is one thing, substantive law another; sale is one contract, hire is quite another contract; the introduction of the contracts of good faith such as sale does not cause the rethinking of the contracts of strict law such as the *stipulatio*.[57] The study of the relations between men (or the state) and the gods is one thing, the study of the relations between men and men quite another.

12 The *Leges Regiae*

As a control on the picture I have drawn of the Twelve Tables and the subsequent development of Roman law, I should like to look, in this final chapter, at what may be learned from the reputed laws of the kings, from Romulus, who founded the city, traditionally in 753 B.C., to the seventh and last king, Tarquin the Proud, who was expelled in 509 B.C. Twin difficulties will be left aside until the end of the chapter: that virtually all scholars deny that the provisions known to us were in fact passed as legislation and that most scholars even regard the rules as later inventions.[1] At this stage we are taking the ancient authors' accounts at face value. Nor need we be overconcerned with the precise meaning of the supposed rules.

If one were to classify the reported provisions into public law, sacred law, private law, and criminal law, then by far the largest group would concern sacred law, the second largest would relate to private law. It would seem that in the time of the kings the religious sphere was not felt to be outside the scope of legal regulation.

More significantly, many provisions cross over and do not fit entirely into one category. It is instructive first to consider the provisions on private law with this fact in mind.

Thus, Romulus, we are told, by one statute induced women to modesty by instituting holy marriage, namely *confarreatio*, in which the wife entered the *manus* of her husband and had, with him, community of property and of the *sacra*.[2] In contrast, if *confarreatio* was mentioned at all in the Twelve Tables, no point was made of the resulting sharing of the religious obligations. Romulus also was responsible for a harsh law that permitted a husband to divorce his wife—but not the wife her husband—for poisoning of offspring (abortion?), tampering with keys (evidence of adultery?), or adultery. A husband who otherwise sent away his wife forfeited half his property to her, and the other half was dedicated to Ceres. A husband who sold his wife was sacrificed to the gods of the underworld.³ If a daughter-in-law struck a parent-in-law she was *sacer* to the gods of the house.⁴

Other provisions of Romulus had no clear connection to religion: that male offspring and firstborn females were to be brought up, and no offspring of less than three years was to be killed unless born monstrous or deformed; that the wife's family, along with her husband, could put her to death for adultery or wine drinking; that a father had complete, lifelong power over a son, could even kill him or sell him, except that after a third sale the son became free from his father.⁵

Numa, the second king, decreed that if a father permitted a son to marry with community of *sacra* and property he could no longer sell his son.⁶ This description of *confarreatio* is again significant. Numa legislated on land boundaries, everyone having to mark the boundaries with stones consecrated to Jupiter Terminus. The obligation to mark boundaries has a secular objective, so their consecration is revealing. Anyone who stole or moved a boundary stone was to be *sacer*.⁷ Numa bestowed private-law privileges on vestal virgins; they were allowed to make a will during the lifetime of their father and were free from tutelage.⁸ Numa also defined periods of mourning, the longest being ten months. During that time a widow could not remarry. If she did she had to sacrifice a pregnant cow.⁹ If someone negligently slew another he had to offer a ram to the victim's agnates.¹⁰ Numa also established workers' guilds which were to have common *sacra* among other things.¹¹ It is plausible to suggest that there was also a religious element in Numa's provision that a pregnant woman who died was not to be buried before the fetus was cut from her.¹²

Tullus Hostilius, the third king, enacted that public aliment would be provided for male triplets until they reached puberty.¹³ Servius Tullius, the sixth king, was responsible for almost fifty laws on contract and delict. He also granted citizenship to freed slaves and enrolled them in the four urban tribes.¹⁴ He further enacted that if a child struck a parent, he was to be *sacer* to the ancestral gods.¹⁵

In addition to the laws just mentioned, the kings were also responsible for much further legislation with religious content or implication. Thus, Romulus, we are told, divided the population into patrician and plebeian, attributing rights and duties to each. The patricians were to be the priests, magistrates, and judges. The plebeians were entrusted to the care of the patricians, and each plebeian could choose a patrician as patron.¹⁶ The patrons were to interpret the law for their clients and bring lawsuits for them. The clients were to help needy patrons to provide a dowry for their daughters, to help with ransom money if the patron or his children were captured by the enemy, and to pay the damages or fines if the patron was condemned in a private or public action. It was against both state law and religious law for either patron or client to accuse the other, give evidence or vote against the other; an offender was guilty of treason, and anyone could lawfully kill him as a victim dedicated to the Jupiter of the underworld.[17] In sharp contrast to the Twelve Tables, the rules here concern sacred, public, and private law; they cross the boundaries between one branch of the law and another; and they make legal distinctions between citizens on the basis of their status. Romulus also distributed political rights unequally to the king, the senate, and the people; and assigned the administration of religious rites to the appropriate persons.[18]

Numa Pompilius was responsible for much legislation that was purely sacred. He decreed that scaleless fish could not be offered as a sacrifice to the gods, and he established the appropriate sacrifices for spoils taken in war.[19] He laid down that wine from a vine that had not been pruned could not be offered as a libation to the gods, and that wine should not be sprinkled on a funeral pyre.[20] A woman who married a man who was already married was forbidden to touch the altar of Juno: if she did, then she had to sacrifice a female lamb, with her hair let down.[21] Restrictions were placed on funerary rites for persons struck by lightning.[22] He also decreed that priests should have their hair cut by bronze, not iron, scissors.[23] Again, he established which days were *fasti*, which *nefasti*.[24] All in all, his legislation on religious matters was, we are told, divided into eight parts, the same number as the colleges of priests.[25]

Tullus Hostilius formulated the legal rules for the declaration of war. He consecrated this law by the fetial rites. (The fetials were a college of priests with ritual obligations for international relationships, especially declarations of war and treaties of peace.)[26] Any war that had not been declared was impious and unjust.[27] Tullus Hostilius also established expiatory rites for incest between brother and sister.[28]

The fourth king, Ancus Marcius, set down the legal formalities, in the control of the fetials, for the declaration of war.[29]

Servius Tullius was active in what we would consider public law. He separated criminal cases from private lawsuits, and he introduced the census with the citizens enrolled in classes and centuries.[30]

Thus goes the story of the laws of the kings as they are set out in the ancient sources. They are vastly different from the law set out in the Twelve Tables. They treat not only private law, but also public and sacred law, two topics excluded from the decemviral code. There is no apparent hesitation in setting down legal differences based on social distinctions between one group of citizens and another. Religion is considerably more prominent in private law than it is in the Twelve Tables.

I have argued elsewhere that there is a pattern to be found in these supposed legal rules that is very plausible for the regal period, and that it is not possible that the rules were transferred by later writers to Rome from some other state, or were invented for some subsequent political reason.[31] Actual legislation, however, cannot be proven, although it is not implausible.[32]

If we can take these supposed legal rules, whether they were actual legislation or not, as representing in a very general way the law before the Twelve Tables, then we see what an extraordinary work that codification is.

The striking characteristics of the code that we have examined appear in even higher relief: absence of public law, absence of sacred law, absence of legal differences between one social group of citizens and another. These characteristics are characteristics not of early Roman law but precisely of the Twelve Tables, and they have to be explained in terms of the circumstances surrounding the promulgation of that code. It was thereafter the very success of the Twelve Tables that gave rise to the system of Roman law that has been so important in world history.

But if no credence is to be given to the picture of law set down for the regal period, then the conclusions are not much changed. Writers such as Dionysius of Halicarnassus, Plutarch, Livy, and Cicero then imagined an early system of law that, as a system, stood in marked contrast to the Twelve Tables. The precisely limited scope of that codification is again emphasized, and the explanation of it has to be the same.

Appendix

The Twelve Tables, their subsequent interpretation, and the development of Roman law pose questions for those interested in the relationship between law and the society in which it operates. I should like to call attention to several issues which, however, have not been explored in this book because they are not germane to the main issues.

1. The promulgation of the Twelve Tables was a direct response to a particular political and social conflict, virtually a revolution. And so was the fact that their interpretation was handed over to the pontiffs. A superficial reading of Livy and Dionysius of Halicarnassus might give the impression that the Twelve Tables represent a victory for the plebs, but this is far from the truth. They did not get what they demanded: knowledge and restriction of the consuls' powers; equality of treatment between one citizen and the next; the very making of this law. Instead, they received what, as far as our sources go, they did not ask for—namely, law on those matters on which the patricians were prepared to grant equality, private law.[1] They did not even get rules on the formulation of the actions or on the calendar days on which it was lawful to bring actions. Further struggle was needed.

The content of the Twelve Tables may well suit a theory that law emerges from the political conditions of society. But that very content dominated all subsequent legal development.

Concessions were wrung, after much further struggle, on legal political rights for plebeians. But there never was comprehensive legislation on constitutional law. Nor was it ever an important intellectual concern of the jurists. Indeed, the view is often expressed that Roman constitutional law did not exist until it was invented by Theodor Mommsen in his classic *Römisches Staatsrecht*, whose publication began in 1871.[2] In contrast, the great success story of the development of Roman law was precisely with regard to the contents of the Twelve Tables. How are we to understand this? Should we say that the success of Roman private law was because of its being written down in the fundamental compilation of the Twelve Tables? If so, we would be saying that historical events cast long shadows. If the Twelve Tables had been promulgated at a different time in the struggle, when the contenders had different priorities, would the shape of Roman law in all time to come have been very different? If there had been no Twelve Tables, would there ever have been a science of law at Rome?

2. But interpretation of the Twelve Tables was handed over to the College of Pontiffs. Only this part of Roman law was to develop mightily. Only Roman private law was to be elaborated. This elaboration could not be without significance. Even for later ages, with the Reception, private law—specifically in the Roman sense—was to be a separate subject from public law. The *ius commune*, the common core of law in Europe, was to be only private law.[3]

To illustrate the long shadow cast by the Twelve Tables, we may take note of basic classification in the numerous "institutes of local law" modeled on Justinian's *Institutes* that appeared in the seventeenth and eighteenth centuries. To take a typical—if the most famous—example of Hugo Grotius's *Inleiding tot de Hollandsche rechtsgeleertheyd* (Introduction to the jurisprudence of Holland), written between 1619 and 1621, first published in 1631:

> All law is public or private.
>
> Public law is the law relating to religion, the conduct of peace and war, the supreme authority and the boundaries of the land, the method of making laws and granting privileges, the punishment of crime and the offices relevant thereto.[4]

Thus, the main division is into public law and private law. Sacred law is firmly classed as part of public law. He continues:

> Private law we shall now proceed to discuss in its parts. Public law is more relevant and important but it is better to begin with private law, because it is older than public law.[5]

Public law, and sacred law as part of it, never reappears in Grotius's *Inleiding*, nor in numerous similar works, just as public law (and religious law) are excluded from the Twelve Tables.[6]

3. The pontiffs did not transfer to law the characteristic features of Roman religion but, probably unconsciously, they used the same modes of reasoning. In arriving at a decision they excluded issues of social or political or economic utility: the arguments were self-contained. The result was "black-letter" law, an autonomous system which appears not to be result oriented. A consequence was a system with sharply defined institutions: sale was one contract, hire was

another; an action on sale would succeed only if there was a contract of sale. The intellectual impact of this was such that it transcended the demise of the Roman world. This approach reappeared with the Reception and dominated legal interpretation.[7] It has been overcome only in this century, and then only in the United States, with such innovations as the Brandeis brief and the "Law and Economics" approach to judicial decision making.

4. But this pontifical reasoning that developed Roman private law had a further impact than simply shaping subsequent approaches to interpretation. Without it, or with a different mode of argumentation, Roman law could not so easily have been borrowed. There would have been no Reception. A foreign rule or institution cannot so easily be borrowed if it is expressly based on unacceptable arguments. It appears too alien. But Roman legal rules, as a result of pontifical reasoning, were not (and could not be) expressly based on Roman religion, Roman ideas of morality, Roman political theory, or Roman economic conditions.

5. More speculatively, one might ask, what if, as the result of the struggle between the orders with a slightly different outcome, the interpretation of the Twelve Tables had been given to persons other than the pontiffs?

6. An underlying theme of this book has been that the style, the sense, of Western private law, especially of continental European law, was a by-product of a very particular political conflict. The Twelve Tables and their pontifical interpretation set the scene for all that was to come. But the Twelve Tables were no objective codification. For political reasons connected with their promulgation, they contained nothing on public, including sacred, law. Similarly, for political reasons connected with their promulgation, the College of Pontiffs was given the sole right of interpretation. This right fixed both the notion of authority for lawmaking and also of legal reasoning. The particular rules of the Twelve Tables might be superseded, but not the idea of what was "real" law or of how it was to be approached.

Notes

Preface

1. Some works, however, do discuss the relationship between *ius* (law) and *fas* (what is religiously proper) in very early Rome. See, e.g., P. Noailles, *Fas et Jus Etudes de droit romain* (Paris, 1948); *Du droit sacré au droit civil* (Paris, 1949); M. Kaser, *Das altrömische Ius* (Göttingen, 1949); H. van den Brink, *Ius Fasque* (Amsterdam, 1968).

2. See, e.g., Cicero, *De haruspicum responsis* 9.19; *De natura deorum* 2.3.8; Sallust, *Bellum Catilinae* 12.3; *Bellum Jugurthinum* 14.19; Valerius Maximus, 1.1.8, 9; Tertullian, *Apologeticus* 25.2; Polybius, 6.56.6ff. Augustine pokes fun at this notion in *De civitate Dei* 4.8; cf., e.g., Wissowa, *Religion und Kultus*, pp. 386ff.; W. H. C. Frend, *Martyrdom and Persecution in the Early Church* (New York, 1967), pp. 77f.

3. Nicolet, with characteristic frankness, says in his *World of the Citizen* (from which I have learned a great deal): "It may cause misgiving that nothing is said on the important subject of religion. No one who has read Fustel de Coulanges can ignore the religious dimension of civic affairs. But this vast subject, privileged as it is by our sources and by contemporary scholarship, is foreign to my tastes and abilities and it is best to admit the fact openly" (p. 15). Sadly I have come belatedly to believe that Roman religion is foreign to the tastes of most Roman lawyers and political historians, and their disciplines have suffered accordingly. Jerzy Linderski kindly provides me with an explanation of this neglect. He writes in a private communication: "It stems from a tradition that either dismissed all religions as irrelevant superstitions or dismissed particularly the religions of antiquity as 'pagan' and hence of no consequence."

4. See A. Watson, "Roman Private Law and the *Leges Regiae*," *Journal of Roman Studies* 82 (1972): 100f.; A. Watson, "*Enuptio gentis*," in *Daube Noster*, ed. A. Watson (Edinburgh, 1974), pp. 331ff.; Watson, *XII Tables*, pp. 166ff.; A. Watson, "The Death of Horatia," *Classical Quarterly* 29 (1979): 436ff. For a very different view of the accuracy of the sources but one which accepts that much can be ascertained for law and religion, see now, Mitchell, *Patricians and Plebeians*.

Introduction

1. Cf., e.g., J. A. North, *C.A.H.* 7.2, pp. 588f.

Chapter 1. Prolegomena on Roman Religion

1. For a recent account illuminating the problems for knowing early Roman religion, see J. A. North, *C.A.H.* 7.2, pp. 573ff.
2. Frequently, it is the detail that seems not to fit or is surprising that enables one to paint a persuasive picture.
3. The framework emerged, of course, only after most of the work on the interaction of law and religion was complete.
4. But it should be stressed that the arguments in this book do not depend on an Indo-European origin of Roman religion.
5. See, above all, Dumézil, *Religion* 1:47ff.
6. Occasional details permit a glimpse of an original mythology shared with other Indo-European people. See Dumézil, *Religion* 1:283ff.
7. See, e.g., A. Momigliano, *C.A.H.* 7.2, p. 108.
8. Latte, who will not speculate on the prehistory of Roman religion, believes the sober coolness of early Roman religion corresponded to something in the deepest Roman character: *Religionsgeschichte*, p. 25. But we should not overlook the rich variety of minor Roman deities. The range of these for early Rome emerges incidentally in J. N. Humphrey, *Roman Circuses* (Berkeley, 1986), pp. 60ff. Nor in stressing the "coolness" of Roman state religion should one overlook the various vigorous private rights, *sacra privata* (which also formed part of pontifical religion), and the vivid celebrations involving a substantial proportion of the whole population, such as the *supplicationes, lustratio, ambarvalia, lectisternia*, and the *ludi*, which had primarily a religious character.
9. *De civitate Dei* 2.4: "Dii autem illi . . . cultores suos ad bene vivendum quare nullis legibus adiuverunt? Utique dignum erat ut, quo modo isti illorum sacra, ita illi istorum facta curarent."
10. See, e.g., M. Krygier, "Critical Legal Studies and Social Theory: A Response to Alan Hunt," *Oxford Journal of Legal Studies* 7 (1987): 26ff.
11. See, e.g., Dumézil, *Religion* 1:283ff.
12. See Dionysius of Halicarnassus, 6.17; 6.94.3; cf. Latte, *Religionsgeschichte*, pp. 161ff. The temple was vowed three years previously by the dictator Aulus Postumius when his army was short of food.
13. J. Linderski rightly stresses that the Romans clearly distinguished between *ius sacrum* and *ius augurale* ("The Augural Law," in *Aufstieg und Niedergang der römischen Welt* vol. 2, book 16, part 3, ed. H. Temporini and W. Haase (Berlin, 1986), pp. 2146ff., at p. 2147. For convenience, however, I will use "sacred law" as an all-embracing term.
14. See, e.g., Momigliano, *C.A.H.* 7.2, p. 108. Linderski properly stresses that the functions were carried out with *scientia*, that is, with research. The rituals were not divinely revealed but resulted from inquiry into what had been found to influence the gods in the way one wished ("The Augural Law," pp. 2226ff.).

Notes to Pages 5–7

15. A good account of the overall situation is in Latte, *Religionsgeschichte*, pp. 18ff.

16. See, e.g., Wissowa, *Religion und Kultus*, pp. 18ff., 389f. That the divine was in everything is not to be seen as an indicator of folk religion.

17. See, e.g., Mitchell, *Patricians and Plebians*, pp. 72f. For the College of Augurs, *collegium augurum*, see Wissowa, *Religion und Kultus*, pp. 523ff.; Linderski, "The Augural Law," pp. 2151ff.

18. See, e.g., Wissowa, *Religion und Kultus*, pp. 501f.; Mitchell, *Patricians and Plebeians*, pp. 65ff.

19. See, e.g., Wissowa, *Religion und Kultus*, p. 503; Latte, *Religionsgeschichte*, pp. 149ff., 195ff., 400ff.; G. J. Szemler, *The Priests of the Roman Republic* (Brussels, 1972), p. 22.

20. See, e.g., Dumézil, *Religion* 1:172.

21. See, e.g., Wissowa, *Religion und Kultus*, p. 504.

22. See, e.g., Latte, *Religionsgeschichte*, p. 23.

23. See, e.g., Wissowa, *Religion und Kultus*, pp. 504ff. The flamines will not be prominent in this book. But the flamen Dialis especially was subject to taboos which go back to the Bronze Age and have no counterpart for the *rex sacrorum* or the *pontifex maximus*; see, e.g., Latte, *Religionsgeschichte*, pp. 36ff., 202f.; P. Braun, "Les Tabous des *feriae*," *L'Anné Sociologique*, 1959:49ff.

24. For the calendar, see especially, Michels, *Calendar*. Discussing their activities, J. A. North rightly says, "To the modern observer, this procedure makes the priests look rather like a constitutional sub-committee of the senate, but this may be misleading: if the priests could not act, they were accepted as supreme authorities on the sacred law in their area. Once the senate had consulted them, it seems inconceivable that their advice should not be followed: *C.A.H.* 7.2, p. 590.

25. And authority over the other priests: Cicero, *Philippicae* 11.8.18; Livy, 38.51.1–5; 40.42.8–10. For the Vestal Virgins see, e.g., North, *C.A.H.* 7.2, pp. 607f.

26. For their general jurisdiction here see Latte, *Religionsgeschichte*, pp. 197f.

27. See, e.g., Schulz, *Legal Science*, p. 17.

28. *De verborum significatu*, p. 113.

29. See Szemler, *Priests*, p. 23.

30. But when a calamity struck, showing divine displeasure, an investigation was held into the cause of the gods' wrath, and in this case the pontiffs were concerned with the facts.

31. See the decree from Tarracina: *C.I.L.* 10.2.985, no. 8259; Bruns, *Fontes*, p. 249. This is properly a cautelary *responsum*.

32. *Ad Atticum* 4.2.3.

33. *De domo sua*.

34. *Ad Atticum* 4.2.23. For other priestly judicial decrees see Livy, 5.25.7; 34.44.2; 8.23.14 (of the *augures*); 31.8.3 (of the fetials).

35. See, e.g., Schulz, *Legal Science*, pp. 16f.

36. Livy, 27.25.7: "Marcellum aliae atque aliae obiectae animo religiones tenebant, in quibus quod cum bello Gallico ad Clastidium aedem Honori et Virtuti vovisset dedicatio eius a pontificibus impediebatur, [8.] quod negabant unam cellam amplius quam uni deo recte dedicari, quia si de caelo tacta aut prodigii aliquid in ea factum esset difficilis procuratio foret, [9.] quod utri deo res divina fieret sciri non posset; neque enim duobus nisi certis deis rite una hostia fieri. Ita addita Virtutis aedes adproperato opere; neque tamen ab ipso aedes eae dedicatae sunt. Tum demum ad exercitum quem priore anno Venusiae reliquerat cum supplemento proficiscitur."

37. Livy, 31.9.5: "Cum dilectum consules haberent pararentque quae ad bellum opus essent, civitas religiosa, in principiis maxime novorum bellorum, [6.] supplicationibus habitis iam et obsecratione circa omnia pulvinaria facta, ne quid praetermitteretur quod aliquando factum esset, ludos Iovi donumque vovere consulem, cui provincia Macedonia evenisset, iussit. [7.] Moram voto publico Licinius pontifex maximus attulit, qui negavit ex incerta pecunia vovere licere; ex certa voveri debere, quia ea pecunia non posset in bellum usui esse seponique statim deberet nec cum alia pecunia misceri; quod si factum esset, votum rite solvi non posse. [8.] Quamquam et res et auctor movebat, tamen ad collegium pontificum referre consul iussus, si posset recte votum incertae pecuniae suscipi. [9.] Posse rectiusque etiam esse pontifices decreverunt. [10.] Vovit in eadem verba consul praeeunte maximo pontifice quibus antea quinquennalia vota suscipi solita erant, praeterquam quod tanta pecunia quantam tum cum solveretur senatus censuisset, ludos donaque facturum vovit. Octiens ante ludi magni de certa pecunia voti erant; hi primi de incerta."

38. It is worth noting in passing that one of the most important of the Roman actions, the *condictio*, could at first be brought (as a result of the *lex Silia*) only where what was claimed was a fixed sum of money, then (as a result of the *lex Calpurnia*) when what was claimed was a determinate thing (*G.* 4.19). The dates of these statutes are quite uncertain, but since they granted the archaic form of action, the *legis actio*, and since the newer form of action, the *formula*, was available for the *condictio* by 184 B.C. (for the argument see A. Watson, *Roman Private Law Around 200 B.C.* [Edinburgh, 1971], pp. 126f.), they will have introduced the *condictio* where the claim was for something certain by 200 B.C., which is the date relevant for the events recorded by Livy. Only much later was the *condictio* available when the claim was for an *incertum*, that is, not a fixed sum or specific thing; cf., e.g., Kaser, *Privatrecht* 1:198f. I am not suggesting that the requirement (until 200 B.C.) that a *votum* (vow) had to be for a *certum* influenced the original scope of the *condictio*, or vice versa—only that they illustrate the same pattern of thought.

39. *Saturnalia* 1.16.25: "Sed et Fabius Maximus Servilianus pontifex in libro duodecimo negat oportere atro die parentare, quia tunc quoque Janum Jovemque praefari necesse est, quos nominari atro die non oportet."

40. This is inscribed on two pillars:

Notes to Pages 9–10

I	II
[D(is)] M(anibus).	[eximere et i] *ter-*
[C]*collegi-*	[um ex] *pra-*
[u]*m pon*[ti-	[escr]*ipto*
f]*icum* [de]-	[d]*eponer*
5 *crevit, si e-*	5 *e et script-*
a ita sunt	*uram titu-*
que libelo	*li at prist-*
[c]*ontene-*	*inam for-*
ntur, pla-	*mam rest-*
10 *cere per*	10 *ituere pia-*
[mitte] *re*¹ *puela-*	*culo prius*
[m, de] *q(ua) agatu-*	*dato operi-*
[r, s]*acelo*	*s faciend-*
	i ove atra.

C.I.L. 10.2.985, no. 8259; Bruns, *Fontes*, p. 249. For other instances in which it seems the pontiffs gave no reasons for their *responsum*, see Livy, 5.25.7; 34.44.2. This may also be true of Coruncanius in Pliny, *Historia naturalis* 8.77.206. For an occasion when the augurs seem to have given no reasons, Livy, 8.23.14.

41. *C.I.L.* 6.2, no. 10675: "Aelius Dignus, Paccius Charito et socii hoc cepotaphium muro cinctum cum suo iure omni ex auctoritate et iudicio pontificum possiderunt." For other inscriptions, see Bruns, *Fontes*, pp. 385f. For another cautelary *responsum* of the pontiffs, see Tacitus, *Annales* 1.10; of the fetials, Livy, 31.8.3.

42. See the information and texts about Q. Fabius Pictor, P. Licinius Crassus, Q. Fabius Maximus Servilianus, L. Furius Philus, P. Mucius Scaevola, Q. Mucius Scaevola, L. Iulius Caesar, Manilius, Octavius Hersennius, M. Terentius Varro, Sextus Papirius, Appius Claudius AP. F. Pulcher, C. Claudius Marcellus, L. Cincius, Granius Flaccus, and M. Valerius Messalla in F. P. Bremer, *Iurisprudentiae Antehadrianae quae supersunt*, vol. 1 (Leipzig, 1896).

43. See, e.g., Wissowa, *Religion und Kultus*, pp. 479f.

44. On this paragraph see, e.g., Jolowicz and Nicholas, *Introduction*, pp. 9ff., 30ff.; H. Volkmann, in *Der Kleine Pauly* 4:551f. (s.v. *patres, patricii*), 4:919ff. (s.v. *plebs*), 5:105ff. (s.v. *senatus*); Wieacker, *Rechtsgeschichte* 1:229ff., 354ff.; Talamanca, *Lineamenti*, pp. 51ff.; A. Momigliano, *C.A.H.* 7.2, pp. 101ff.; A. Drummond, *C.A.H.* 7.2, pp. 178ff.; Mitchell, *Patricians and Plebeians*, pp. 131ff. Mitchell very much downplays the struggle between the orders.

45. See, e.g., Szemler, *Priests*.

46. See, e.g., Wissowa, *Religion und Kultus*, p. 487.

47. *De divinatione* 2.36.77: "Nam ex acuminibus quidem, quod totum auspicium

militare est, iam M. Marcellus ille quinquiens consul totum omisit, idem imperator, idem augur optimus. Et quidem ille dicebat, si quando rem agere vellet, ne impediretur auspiciis, lectica operta facere iter se solere. Huic simile est, quod nos augures praecipimus, ne iuge auspicium obveniat ut iumenta iubeant diiungere. Quid est aliud nolle moneri a Iove nisi efficere ut, aut ne fieri possit auspicium, aut, si fiat, videri?" For the taking of the auspices see, e.g., Nicolet, *World of the Citizen*, pp. 250ff.; for prodigies see, e.g., North, *C.A.H.* 7.2, pp. 595f.

48. *Historia naturalis* 28.4.17: "Haec satis sint exemplis ut appareat ostentorum vires et in nostra potestate esse ac prout quaeque accepta sint ita valere. in augurum certe disciplina constat neque diras neque ulla auspicia pertinere ad eos qui quamcumque rem ingredientes observare se ea negaverint, quo munere divinae indulgentiae maius nullum est."

49. Cicero, *De divinatione* 1.15.28; 2.34.72f.

50. See, e.g., Livy, 1.19.4; Polybius, 6.56.6ff.; Cicero, *De legibus* 2.12.31–13.32; 3.19.43; *Philippicae* 2.32.80–3.3.83; Pliny, *Historia naturalis* 28.3.10ff.; Dionysius of Halicarnassus, 2.6. It was also possible for a Roman to insist that it was useful for citizens to believe the gods were the rulers of all things, without there necessarily being an air of cynicism; see, e.g., Cicero, *De legibus* 2.7.15f.

51. See the evidence set out by Liebeschuetz, *Continuity*, pp. 25ff. I am greatly indebted to that book for this section of the chapter.

52. Macrobius, *Saturnalia* 1.16.9: "Affirmabant autem sacerdotes pollui ferias, si indictis conceptisque opus aliquod fieret. Praeterea regem sacrorum flaminesque non licebat videre feriis opus fieri, et ideo per praeconem denuntiabant nequid tale ageretur et praecepti neglegens multabatur. [10.] Praeter multam vero affirmabatur eum qui talibus diebus imprudens aliquid egisset, porco piaculum dare debere. Prudentem expiare non posse Scaevola pontifex asseverebat, sed Umbro negat eum pollui, qui opus vel ad deos pertinens sacrorumve causa fecisset, vel aliquid ad urgentem vitae utilitatem respiciens actitasset. [11.] Scaevola denique consultus quid feriis agi liceret, respondit quod praetermissum noceret. Quapropter si bos in specum decidisset eumque pater familias adhibitis operis liberasset, non est visus ferias polluisse; nec ille qui trabem tecti fractam fulciendo ab imminenti vindicavit ruina."

53. Varro, *De lingua latina* 6.30: "Contrarii horum vocantur dies nefasti, per quos dies nefas fari praetorem 'do,' 'dico,' 'addico'; itaque non potest agi: necesse est aliquo ‹eorum› uti verbo, cum lege qui‹d› peragitur. Quod si tum imprudens id verbum emisit ac quem manumisit, ille nihilo minus est liber, sed vitio, ut magistratus vitio creatus nihilo setius magistratus. Praetor qui tum fatus est, si imprudens fecit, piaculari hostia facta piatur; si prudens dixit, Quintus Mucius aiebat eum expiari ut impium non posse."

54. Latte, *Religionsgeschichte*, p. 203 n. 4.

55. In a private dedication, *lex luci Spoletina*, of a sacred grave, the dedicator establishes a penalty for violations of his rules then sets out a greater penalty for deliberate, knowing violations: *sei quis scies violasit dolo malo* (Bruns, *Fontes*, p. 283).

56. It may be mentioned here in passing that the *stipulatio*, the oldest Roman contract, was valid even if entered into on account of fraud or intimidation.

57. See, e.g., Wissowa, *Religion und Kultus*, pp. 70ff.; Latte, *Religionsgeschichte*, pp. 264ff.; Liebeschuetz, *Continuity*, pp. 1ff. A similar problem of understanding cynicism and belief exists in the otherwise very different world of the great witch-hunts of the later sixteenth and seventeenth centuries. I have learned most from H. C. E. Midelfort, *Witch Hunting in Southwestern Germany, 1562–1684* (Stanford, 1972), and C. Larner, *Enemies of God, The Witch-hunt in Scotland* (Baltimore, 1981).

58. *De divinatione* 1.58.132: "superstitiosi vates inpudentesque harioli, aut inertes aut insani aut quibus egestas imperat; qui sibi semitam non sapiunt, alteri monstrant viam; quibus divitias pollicentur, ab iis drachumam ipsi petunt. De his divitiis sibi deducant drachumam, reddant cetera."

59. *De divinatione* 1.57.131: "nam isti qui linguam avium intellegunt plusque ex alieno iecore sapiunt quam ex suo, magis audiendum quam auscultandum censeo." Cf. Plautus, *Asinaria*, 259ff., and *Mostellaria*, 571.

60. *De divinatione* 2.24.51.

61. "Nil credo auguribus, qui auris verbis deivitant alienas, suas ut auro locupletent domas" (in Nonius 95.6, s.v. *Deivitant*). For augural law see, e.g., *Catalano Contributi allo Studio del Diritto Augurale* 1 (Turin, 1960); Linderski, "Augural Law."

62. Suetonius, *Divus Julius* 13; Plutarch, *Caesar* 7.29.

63. Cf., e.g., North, *C.A.H.* 7.2, p. 588.

64. Cf. Liebeschuetz, *Continuity*, p. 22; Wardman, *Religion*, pp. 42ff.

65. See the very revealing remark on the occasion of the Bacchanalia in Livy, 39.15.11.

66. See, e.g., Michels, *Calendar*, pp. 36ff.

67. *D.* 1.1.1.2; cf., e.g., Wissowa, *Religion und Kultus*, p. 380.

68. *De civitate Dei* 4.27: "Relatum est in litteras doctissimum pontificem Scaevolam disputasse tria genera tradita deorum: unum a poetis, alterum a philosophis, tertium a principibus civitatis. primum genus nugatorium dicit esse, quod multa de diis fingantur indigna; secundum non congruere civitatibus, quod habeat aliqua supervacua, aliqua etiam quae obsit populis nosse."

69. Livy 4.7.3; 5.17; 6.27.5; 6.38.9f.; 8.15.6; 8.17.4; 8.29–37 (a *vitium*, but deposition did not occur); 9.7.13f.; 10.47.1; 22.33.12; 23.19.3 (a retaking of the auspices); 23.31.13; cf. Liebeschuetz, *Continuity*, p. 209.

70. See Liebeschuetz, *Continuity*, p. 13 n. 2.

71. See the list given by A. W. Lintott, *Violence in Republican Rome* (Oxford, 1968), pp. 135f. For the political importance of the *augures* because of the auspices, see, e.g., North, *C.A.H.* 7.2, p. 585.

Chapter 2. The Twelve Tables: Contents

1. Festus, s.v. *Diffareatio*; Plutarch, *Quaestiones Romanae*, 50.
2. For the argument see Watson, *XII Tables*, pp. 9ff. But that *confarreatio* was mentioned at all is regarded as doubtful; see, e.g., Kaser, *Privatrecht* 1:76 n. 1; for E. Volterra, "Nuove ricerche sulla 'conventio in manum,'" *Memorie della Accademia dei Lincei* 1966:283 n. 64, the hypothesis is plausible but the arguments rather weak; for Linderski, correctly, the common tradition of formulation on which the hypothesis rests cannot be traced back beyond Ateius Capito, who died in A.D. 22 ("*Usu, farre coemptione*, Bemerkungen zur Ueberlieferung eines Rechtsatzes," *ZSS* 100 [1984]: 301ff.).
3. See, in the first instance, D. Daube, "Texts and Interpretation in Roman and Jewish Law," *Jewish Journal of Sociology* 3 (1961): 3ff.
4. See Watson, *Law Making*, pp. 143ff.
5. He also apparently does not deal with any statutory law subsequent to the *lex Aquilia* of around 287 B.C.
6. Livy, 4.1.1, 2; 4.4.5–12; 4.5.5; 4.6.2; Dionysius of Halicarnassus, 10.60.5; Cicero, *De re publica* 2.37.63.
7. See, e.g., Watson, *XII Tables*, p. 20. The ban, which was regarded as a grievance by the plebs, was removed by the *lex Canuleia* as early as 445 B.C. Significantly, the ban could be an inconvenience only for the most prominent plebeian families.
8. See Watson, *XII Tables*, pp. 38f.
9. *Collatio* 10.7.11; cf. Watson, *Evolution of Law*, pp. 10ff.
10. See Watson, *XII Tables*, pp. 92f.
11. D. 40.1.25; 40.1.29.1; *Epitome Ulpiani* 2.4.
12. See Watson, *XII Tables*, pp. 52ff.
13. See Watson, *XII Tables*, p. 156.
14. Six rules, though not necessarily six separate provisions: Cicero, *Topica* 4.23, *Pro Caecina* 19.54, *De officiis* 1.12.37, and *De legibus* 1.21.55 and 2.24.61; G. 2.42, 45, 47, 49, 54, 204; D. 41.3.33pr.; J. 2.6.2; see A. Watson, "The Origins of *Usus*," *RIDA* 23 (1976): 265ff.
15. Also for the acquisition of *manus*, see Watson, "*Usus*," pp. 269f.
16. See Watson, "*Usus*," p. 266.
17. These are now collected in Tab. 8.
18. Wieacker suggests that the accepted proportion of survival of one-third may be too conservative (*Rechtsgeschichte* 1:289). I agree and would rate the survival rate much higher. R. Westbrook, "The Nature and Origins of the Twelve Tables," *ZSS* 118 (1988): 74ff., is of interest only for its bibliography. For the preservation of the Twelve Tables, see, e.g., A. Drummond, *C.A.H.* 7.2, p. 115.
19. See, e.g., W. Strzelecki, in *Der Kleine Pauly* 2:727f.
20. See also Wieacker, *Rechtsgeschichte* 1:290f.; Talamanca, *Lineamenti*, pp. 99ff.
21. *De legibus* 2.4.9.
22. See Watson, *Law Making*, pp. 134ff.

23. See the reconstruction and sources in Bruns, *Fontes*, pp. 8f. On the nature of such laws, see below, chap. 12.
24. *G.* 1.144f.
25. Livy, 3.9.1ff.
26. Though the private-law provisions in the laws of the kings contain more religious elements; see chap. 12.
27. Criminal law is treated in Tabs. 8.1, 8, 9, 10, 14, 21, 23, 34; 9.3, 4, 5. But the boundary line between private law and criminal law should be regarded as indistinct. Criminal law does not really fall within the Roman concept of public law, and it is even treated, though briefly, in Justinian's *Institutes*, which is otherwise concerned wholly with private law and actions (*J.* 4.18). Disposal of the dead is discussed in Tab. 10.
28. Tab. 8.1: see the sources and authorities in *FIRA* 1:52; cf. A. D. Manfredini, *La Diffamazione verbale nel Diritto Romano* (Milan, 1979), pp. 1ff.
29. Tab. 8.8; see *FIRA* 1:55f. For an example of a trial conducted by an aedile, see Pliny, *Historia naturalis* 18.41–43. Some scholars hold there is a magic element in the search (in Tab. 8.15) *lance et licio* for stolen property; see, e.g., Wieacker, *Rechtsgeschichte*, p. 245.
30. Tab. 8.9; *FIRA* 1:56.
31. Tab. 8.21; *FIRA* 1:62. What this penalty meant at the time of the Twelve Tables is uncertain.
32. Tab. 8.24; *FIRA* 1:62f; see C. A. Melis, "*Arietem offerre*," *Labeo* 34 (1988): 135ff.
33. *D.* 44.6.3; Tab. 12.4; *FIRA* 1:73.
34. Wieacker stresses the profane character of the Twelve Tables (*Rechtsgeschichte*, p. 290).
35. Exod. 20.12.
36. A very similar provision is to be found in the new *Nederlands Burgerlijk Wetboek*, the Dutch civil code, at art. 245.1 (replacing art. 355.1 of the old code): "Een kind, van welke leeftijd ook, is aan zijn ouders eerbied en outzag verschuldigd" (A child of any age whatsoever owes his parents respect and honor). Commentators have remarked that only with difficulty can this be regarded as a legal rule, with a legal content, and there is no sanction; see, e.g., E. A. A. Luijten, *Het personen- en familierecht in het nieuwe burgerlijk wetboek* (Zwolle, 1977), p. 258 (by W. H. A. Jonkers); A. Pitlo, *Het Nederlands Burgerlijk Wetboek*, 1, *Het Personen- en Familierecht*, 7th ed. by G. R. Van der Burght and M. Rood-de Boer (Arnhem, 1985), p. 448 (by Rood-de Boer).

Chapter 3. The Twelve Tables: The Public/Private Law Distinction

1. This is not to suggest that the distinction public/private was not also being made in classical Athens, and that behavior might not there be punished more severely be-

cause it affected the public: see, e.g., D. Cohen, "Work in Progress: The Enforcement of Morals: An Historical Perspective," *Rechtshistorisches Journal* 3 (1984): 114ff.

2. Cicero, *De oratore* 1.46.201, and *Divinatio in Caecilium* 5.18. Still, this is much earlier than some scholars would have us believe. M. J. Horwitz, for instance, would date it to the sixteenth century and relates it to the emergence of nation-states and theories of sovereignty, and he also sees it as a reaction to claims of monarchs (and later, parliaments) to unrestrained power ("The History of the Public/Private Distinction," *University of Pennsylvania Law Review* 130 [1982]: 1423ff.).

3. On the Edict, see Lenel, *Edictum*; on Quintus Mucius's commentary on the *ius civile*, see Watson, *Law Making*, pp. 143ff.

4. See, e.g., A. Drummond, *C.A.H.* 7.2, pp. 114f., 227ff.

5. For the plebeian movement, see, e.g., Drummond, *C.A.H.* 7.2, pp. 212ff. Mitchell is skeptical about the publication of the Twelve Tables: *Patricians and Plebeians*, pp. 122ff.

6. Livy, 3.9.1: "Sic res Romana in antiquum statum rediit, secundaeque belli res exemplo urbanos motus excitaverunt. [2.] C. Terentilius Harsa tribunus plebis eo anno fuit. Is consulibus absentibus ratus locum tribuniciis actionibus datum, per aliquot dies patrum superbiam ad plebem criminatus, maxime in consulare imperium tamquam nimium nec tolerable liberae civitati invehebatur; [3.] nomine enim tantum minus invidiosum, re ipsa prope atrocious quam regium esse; [4.] quippe duos pro uno dominos acceptos, immoderata, infinita potestate, qui soluti atque effrenati ipsi omnes metus legum omniaque supplicia verterent in plebem. [5.] quae ne aeterna illis licentia sit, legem se promulgaturum ut quinque viri creentur legibus de imperio consulari scribendis; quod populus in se ius dederit, eo consulem usurum, non ipsos libidinem ac licentiam suam pro lege habituros."

7. Livy, 3.10.5ff.

8. See, e.g., Livy, 3.11.3, 9, 12, 13; 3.15.1; 3.18.6.

9. Livy, 3.19.11.

10. Livy, 3.31.5ff.

11. Scholars generally exclude the idea of an embassy to Athens, but contact with Greek legal notions (from Magna Graecia) is not implausible. For very different views on the extent of such influence (which need not detain us here), see, e.g., Wieacker, *Rechtsgeschichte* 1:300ff., and A. Watson, *Legal Transplants: An Approach to Comparative Law* (Edinburgh, 1974), pp. 25ff.

12. Livy, 3.32.1.

13. Livy 3.32.5: "Inde consules C. Menenius P. Sestius Capitolinus. Neque eo anno quicquam belli externi fuit: domi motus orti. [6.] Iam redierant legati cum Atticis legibus. Eo intentius instabant tribuni ut tandem scribendarum legum initium fieret. Placet creari decemviros sine provocatione, et ne quis eo anno alius magistratus esset. [7.] Admiscerenturne plebeii controuersia aliquamdiu fuit; postremo concessum patribus, modo ne lex Icilia de Aventino aliaéque sacratae leges abrogarentur." Strangely,

Jolowicz and Nicholas, *Introduction*, p. 13, claim that plebeians were eligible to be *decemviri*.

14. Livy, 3.31f.; Dionysius of Halicarnassus, 10.31f.
15. The overall consistency of the sources on the legislative history of the Twelve Tables is noted by Wieacker, *Rechtsgeschichte* 1:287.
16. Dionysius of Halicarnassus, 10.1.1: Μετὰ δὲ τούτους ὀλυμπιὰς μὲν ἦν ὀγδοηκοστή, ἣν ἐνίκα στάδιον Τορύμβας Θεσσαλός, ἄρχοντος 'Αθήνησι Φρασικλέους· ὕπατοι δὲ ἀπεδείχθησαν ἐν Ῥώμῃ Πόπλιος Οὐολούμνιος καὶ Σερούιος [1] Σολπίκιος Καμερῖνος.[2] οὗτοι στρατιὰν μὲν οὐδεμίαν ἐξήγαγον οὔτε ἐπὶ τιμωρίας ἀναπράξει τῶν ἀδικούντων σφᾶς τε αὐτοὺς καὶ τοὺς συμμάχους οὔθ' ὡς διὰ φυλακῆς τὰ οἰκεῖα ἕξοντες· τῶν δ' ἐντὸς τείχους κακῶν πρόνοιαν ἐποιοῦντο, μή τι δεινὸν ὁ δῆμος ἐπὶ τῇ βουλῇ συστὰς ἐξεργάσηται. [2.] ἐταράττετο γὰρ αὖθις ὑπὸ τῶν δημάρχων ἀναδιδασκόμενος ὅτι πολιτειῶν κρατίστη τοῖς ἐλευθέροις ἐστὶν ἡ [3] ἰσηγορία, καὶ κατὰ νόμους ἠξίου διοικεῖσθαι τά τε ἰδιωτικὰ καὶ τὰ δημόσια. οὔπω γὰρ τότε ἦν οὔτ' ἰσονομία παρὰ Ῥωμαίοις οὔτ' ἰσηγορία, οὐδ' ἐν γραφαῖς ἅπαντα τὰ δίκαια τεταγμένα· ἀλλὰ τὸ μὲν ἀρχαῖον οἱ βασιλεῖς αὐτῶν ἔταττον τοῖς δεομένοις τὰς δίκας, καὶ τὸ δικαιωθὲν ὑπ' ἐκείνων τοῦτο νόμος ἦν. [3.] ὡς δ' ἐπαύσαντο μοναρχούμενοι, τοῖς κατ' ἐνιαυτὸν ὑπατεύουσιν ἀνέκειτο τά τε ἄλλα τῶν βασιλέων ἔργα καὶ ἡ τοῦ δικαίου διάγνωσις, καὶ τοῖς ἀμφισβητοῦσι πρὸς ἀλλήλους ὑπὲρ ὁτουδήτινος ἐκεῖνοι τὰ δίκαια οἱ διαιροῦντες ἦσαν. [4.] τούτων δὲ τὰ μὲν πολλὰ τοῖς τρόποις [1] τῶν ἀρχόντων ἀριστίνδην ἀποδεικνυμένων ἐπὶ τὰς ἀρχὰς ἀκόλουθα ἦν· κομιδῇ δ' ὀλίγα τινὰ ἐν ἱεραῖς ἦν βύβλοις ἀποκείμενα, ἃ νόμων εἶχε δύναμιν, ὧν οἱ πατρίκιοι τὴν γνῶσιν εἶχον μόνοι διὰ τὰς ἐν ἄστει διατριβάς, οἱ δὲ πολλοὶ ἐμπορευόμενοί τε καὶ γεωργοῦντες διὰ πολλῶν ἡμερῶν εἰς ἄστυ καταβαίνοντες ἐπὶ τὰς ἀγορὰς ἄπειροι ἔτι ἦσαν. [5.] τὸ δὲ πολίτευμα τοῦτο πρῶτος μὲν ἐπείρασεν εἰσαγαγεῖν Γάιος Τερέντιος [2] δημαρχῶν ἐν τῷ παρελθόντι ἔτει, ἀτελὲς δὲ ἠναγκάσθη καταλιπεῖν τοῦ τε πλήθους ὄντος ἐπὶ στρατοπέδων καὶ τῶν ὑπάτων ἐπίτηδες ἐν τῇ πολεμίᾳ γῇ τὰς δυνάμεις κατασχόντων ἕως ὁ τῆς ἀρχῆς αὐτοῖς παρέλθῃ χρόνος.
17. Dionysius of Halicarnassus, 10.2.1.
18. Dionysius of Halicarnassus, 10.3.3: ταῦτα καὶ πολλὰ τούτοις ὅμοια παρ' ἑκατέρων ἐπὶ πολλὰς ἡμέρας ἐλέγετο, καὶ προύβαινε διὰ κενῆς ὁ χρόνος· ἐν ᾧ τῶν κατὰ τὴν πόλιν οὔτε δημοσίων οὔτε ἰδίων οὐδὲν ἐτελεῖτο. ὡς δ' οὐδὲν ἐγίνετο τῶν προὔργου, λόγων μὲν [2] ἐκείνων καὶ κατηγοριῶν ἃς ἐποιοῦντο κατὰ τῆς βουλῆς οἱ δήμαρχοι ἀπέστησαν· συναγαγόντες δὲ τὸ πλῆθος εἰς τὴν [3] ἐκκλησίαν ὑπέσχοντο τῷ δήμῳ νόμον εἰσοίσειν ὑπὲρ ὧν ἠξίουν. ἐπαινέσαντος δὲ τοῦ πλήθους τὸν λόγον οὐδὲν ἔτι ἀναβαλόμενοι [4] τὸν παρασκευασθέντα νόμον ἀνέγνωσαν· κεφάλαια δὲ αὐτοῦ τάδε ἦν· ἄνδρας αἱρεθῆναι δέκα ὑπὸ τοῦ δήμου συναχθείσης ἀγορᾶς ἐννόμου τοὺς πρεσβυτάτους τε καὶ φρονιμωτάτους,[5] οἷς ἐστι πλείστη πρόνοια τιμῆς τε καὶ δόξης ἀγαθῆς· τούτους δὲ συγγράψαντας τοὺς ὑπὲρ ἁπάντων νόμους τῶν τε κοινῶν καὶ τῶν ἰδίων εἰς τὸν δῆμον ἐξενεγκεῖν· τοὺς δὲ συγγραφησομένους ὑπ'

αὐτῶν νόμους ἐκκεῖσθαι [6] ἐν ἀγορᾷ ταῖς καθ' ἕκαστον ἐνιαυτὸν ἀποδειχθησομέναις ἀρχαῖς καὶ τοῖς ἰδιώταις ὅρους τῶν πρὸς ἀλλήλους δικαίων.

19. Dionysius of Halicarnassus, 10.4.

20. Dionysius of Halicarnassus, 10.51.5: κεφάλαιον δ' ἐστὶν ὧν ὑμῖν παραινῶ, πρέσβεις ἑλέσθαι τοὺς μὲν εἰς τὰς Ἑλληνίδας πόλεις τὰς ἐν Ἰταλίᾳ, τοὺς δ' εἰς Ἀθήνας, οἵτινες αἰτησάμενοι παρὰ τῶν Ἑλλήνων τοὺς κρατίστους νόμους καὶ μάλιστα τοῖς ἡμετέροις ἁρμόττοντας βίοις οἴσουσι δεῦρο. ἀφικομένων δ' αὐτῶν τοὺς τότε ὑπάτους προθεῖναι τῇ βουλῇ σκοπεῖν τίνας ἑλέσθαι δεήσει νομοθέτας καὶ ἥντινα ἕξοντας ἀρχὴν καὶ χρόνον ὅσον καὶ τἆλλα, ὅπως ἂν αὐτῇ φαίνηται συνοίσειν, στασιάζειν δὲ μηκέτι πρὸς τὸ δημοτικὸν μηδ' ἄλλας ἐπ' ἄλλαις ἀναιρεῖσθαι συμφοράς, ἄλλως τε καὶ περὶ νόμων φιλονεικοῦντας οἳ κἂν εἰ μηθὲν ἄλλο τήν γέ τοι δόξαν τῆς ἀξιώσεως ἔχουσιν εὐπρεπῆ."

21. Dionysius of Halicarnassus, 10.55.4ff.

22. Perhaps one should believe it was the *comitia centuriata*. In any event, the body responsible for establishing the *decemviri* was controlled by the patricians.

23. The second group of *decemviri* contained plebeians, according to Dionysius of Halicarnassus, 10.58.4; this is contradicted by Livy, 4.3.17.

24. Livy, 3.34.6; Dionysius of Halicarnassus, 10.57.6. For the view that the Twelve Tables were a victory for the patricians, see B. Frier, *Libri Annales Pontificum Maximorum: The Origins of the Annalistic Tradition* (Rome, 1979), pp. 130f.

25. The exceptions, or apparent exceptions, of *res religiosae, confarreatio, adrogatio*, and the making of a will *calatis comitiis*, are discussed in subsequent chapters.

26. See Jolowicz and Nicholas, *Introduction*, p. 109.

27. Some doubts have been expressed as to whether the *comitia centuriata* existed with political functions as early as the Twelve Tables: for views see, e.g., E. S. Stavely, "The Constitution of the Roman Republic, 1940–54," *Historia* 5 (1956): 74ff., at pp. 75ff.; A. Drummond, *C.A.H.* 7.2, pp. 198ff. If the *comitia centuriata* is later, then the provision would relate to the *comitia curiata*.

28. "Privilegia ne inroganto; de capite civis nisi per maximum comitiatum ne ferunto." For these two clauses see Cicero, *De legibus* 3.4.11; 3.19.44; *Pro Sestio* 30.65; *De domo* 17.43; and *De re publica* 2.36.61. The division is, of course, arbitrary and is not to be found in subsequent European law until it gradually reappears with the Reception of Roman law; see, e.g., A. Watson, *The Making of the Civil Law* (Cambridge, Mass., 1981), pp. 144f.

Max Kaser provides a very different explanation for the omission of legal institutions from the Twelve Tables; *Römisches Privatrecht*, 15th ed. (Munich, 1989), p. 15. He writes, "Their principal motivation lies in the struggle between the orders. They were intended to assure to the plebeians legal equality with the patricians, and mainly laid down particular legal issues in which the economically weaker plebeians felt threatened by the patricians in control of courts." Any view that there is an economic basis for the inclusion or omission of rules from the Twelve Tables is flatly contradicted by both the surviving sources and what can be deduced about omitted provisions. Moreover, it is likely that the leaders of the plebs who pressed for the reform were, as later, wealthy, and not weaker economically than many patricians.

29. *D.* 1.2.2.5 (*Manual*, sole book): "His legibus latis coepit (ut naturaliter evenire solet, ut interpretatio desideraret prudentium auctoritatem) necessariam esse disputatione fori. Haec disputatio et hoc ius, quod sine scripto venit compositum a prudentibus, propria parte aliqua non appellatur, ut ceterae partes iuris suis nominibus designantur, datis propriis nominibus ceteris partibus, sed communi nomine appellatur ius civile. [6.] Deinde ex his legibus eodem tempore fere actiones compositae sunt, quibus inter se homines disceptarent: quas actiones ne populus prout vellet institueret, certas sollemnesque esse voluerunt: et appellatur haec pars iuris legis actiones, id est legitimae actiones. et ita eodem paene tempore tria haec iura nata sunt: lege duodecim tabularum ex his fluere coepit ius civile, ex isdem legis actiones compositae sunt. Omnium tamen harum et interpretandi scientia et actiones apud collegium pontificum erant, ex quibus constituebatur, quis quoquo anno praeesset privatis."

30. Cf. Talamanca, *Lineamenti*, pp. 289, 292ff.

31. See Watson, *Law Making*, pp. 151ff.

32. See especially, D. Daube, "On the Third Chapter of the *Lex Aquilia*," *LQR* 52 (1936): 253ff.

33. See, e.g., Watson, *XII Tables*, pp. 71ff.

34. *J.* 1.20.3; cf. J. A. C. Thomas, *The Institutes of Justinian* (Cape Town, 1975), p. 53.

35. For the sources for these statutes see Rotondi, *Leges publicae*, pp. 282ff.

36. The definition of *ius civile* by the later Papinian is much wider (*D.* 1.1.7.1).

37. See Kunkel, *Herkunft*, p. 18.

38. Certainly procedure appears in the early part of the Twelve Tables, but as some understanding of classification developed, Mucius might have removed his treatment to near the end. Gaius devotes the first three books of his *Institutes* to substantive law, the final book to actions. See now, Watson, *Law Making*, pp. 144, 151.

39. *De oratore* 1.46.201; *Divinatio in Caecilium* 5.18.

40. *D.* 1.1.1.2. (*Institutes*, book 1): "Huius studii duae sunt positiones, publicum et privatum. publicum ius est quod ad statum rei Romanae spectat, privatum quod ad singulorum utilitatem: sunt enim quaedam publice utilia, quaedam privatim. publicum ius in sacris, in sacerdotibus, in magistratibus constitit. privatum ius tripertitum est: collectum etenim est ex naturalibus praeceptis aut gentium aut civilibus." Cf. *J.* 1.1.4: on these texts see M. Kaser, ' "Ius publicum" und "ius privatum," ' *ZSS* 116 (1986): 1ff.

41. *D.* 1.1.10 (*Rules*, book 1): "Iustitia est constans et perpetua voluntas ius suum cuique tribuendi. [1.] Iuris praecepta sunt haec: honeste vivere, alterum non laedere, suum cuique tribuere. [2.] Iuris prudentia est divinarum atque humanarum rerum notitia, iusti atque iniusti scientia." Cf. *J.* 1.1pr., 1, 3.

Chapter 4. Formalism in Religion and Law

1. Dionysius of Halicarnassus, 4.59.
2. Dionysius of Halicarnassus, 4.60.1: Τούτοις τοῖς ἀνδράσιν ἀφικομένοις εἰς τὴν οἰκίαν τοῦ τερατοσκόπου περιτυγχάνει τι μειράκιον ἐξιόν, ᾧ φράσαντες ὅτι Ῥωμαίων εἰσὶ πρέσβεις τῷ μάντει βουλόμενοι ἐντυχεῖν,[2] παρεκάλουν ἀπαγγεῖλαι πρὸς αὐτόν. καὶ ὁ νεανίας, " Πατὴρ ἐμός ἐστιν," ἔφησεν, " ᾧ χρῄζετε ἐντυχεῖν·[2] ἀσχολεῖται δὲ κατὰ τὸ παρόν· ἔσται δ' ὑμῖν ὀλίγου χρόνου παρελθεῖν πρὸς αὐτόν. [2.] ἐν ᾧ δ' ἐκεῖνον ἐκδέχεσθε, πρὸς ἐμὲ δηλώσατε περὶ τίνος ἥκετε. περιέσται γὰρ ὑμῖν, εἴ τι μέλλετε διὰ τὴν ἀπειρίαν σφάλλεσθαι κατὰ τὴν ἐρώτησιν, ὑπ' ἐμοῦ διδαχθεῖσι μηδὲν ἐξαμαρτεῖν· μοῖρα δ' οὐκ ἐλαχίστη τῶν ἐν μαντικῇ θεωρημάτων ἐρώτησις ὀρθή." ἐδόκει τοῖς ἀνδράσιν οὕτω ποιεῖν, καὶ λέγουσιν αὐτῷ τὸ τέρας. ὁ δ' ὡς ἤκουσε μικρὸν ἐπισχὼν χρόνον, " Ἀκούσατ'," ἔφησεν, " ἄνδρες Ῥωμαῖοι· τὸ μὲν τέρας ὑμῖν ὁ πατὴρ διελεῖται καὶ οὐδὲν ψεύσεται· μάντει γὰρ οὐ θέμις· ἃ δὲ λέγοντες ὑμεῖς καὶ ἀποκρινόμενοι πρὸς τὰς ἐρωτήσεις ἀναμάρτητοί τε καὶ ἀψευδεῖς ἔσεσθε (διαφέρει γὰρ ὑμῖν προεγνωκέναι ταῦτα) παρ' ἐμοῦ μάθετε. [3.] ὅταν ἀφηγήσησθε αὐτῷ τὸ τέρας, οὐκ ἀκριβῶς μανθάνειν φήσας ὅ τι λέγετε περιγράψει τῷ σκήπωνι τῆς γῆς μέρος ὅσον δή τι· ἔπειθ' ὑμῖν ἐρεῖ, ' Τουτὶ μέν ἐστιν ὁ Ταρπήιος λόφος, μέρος δ' αὐτοῦ τουτὶ μὲν τὸ πρὸς τὰς ἀνατολὰς βλέπον, τουτὶ δὲ τὸ πρὸς τὰς δύσεις, βόρειον δ' αὐτοῦ τόδε καὶ τοὐναντίον νότιον.' [4.] ταῦτα τῷ σκήπωνι δεικνὺς πεύσεται παρ' ὑμῶν ἐπὶ ποίῳ τῶν μερῶν τούτων εὑρέθη ἡ κεφαλή. τί οὖν ὑμῖν ἀποκρίνασθαι παραινῶ; μὴ συγχωρεῖν ἐν μηδενὶ τῶν τόπων τούτων, οὓς ἂν ἐκεῖνος τῷ σκήπωνι δεικνὺς πυνθάνηται, τὸ τέρας εὑρεθῆναι, ἀλλ' ἐν Ῥώμῃ φάναι παρ' ὑμῖν[2] ἐν Ταρπηίῳ λόφῳ. ταύτας ἐὰν φυλάττητε τὰς ἀποκρίσεις καὶ μηδὲν παράγησθε ὑπ' αὐτοῦ, συγγνοὺς ὅτι τὸ χρεὼν οὐκ ἔνεστι μετατεθῆναι, διελεῖται τὸ τέρας ὑμῖν ὅ τι βούλεται σημαίνειν καὶ οὐκ ἀποκρύψεται."
[61.1.] Ταῦτα μαθόντες οἱ πρέσβεις, ἐπειδὴ σχολὴν ὁ πρεσβύτης[3] ἔσχε καὶ προῆλθέ τις αὐτοὺς μετιών, εἰσελθόντες φράζουσι τῷ μάντει τὸ τέρας. σοφιζομένου δ' αὐτοῦ καὶ διαγράφοντος ἐπὶ τῆς γῆς περιφερεῖς τε γραμμὰς καὶ ἑτέρας αὖθις εὐθείας καὶ καθ' ἓν ἕκαστον χωρίον ποιουμένου τὰς ὑπὲρ τῆς εὑρέσεως ἐρωτήσεις, οὐδὲν ἐπιταραττόμενοι τὴν γνώμην οἱ πρέσβεις τὴν αὐτὴν ἐφύλαττον ἀπόκρισιν, ὥσπερ αὐτοῖς ὁ τοῦ μάντεως ὑπέθετο υἱός, τὴν Ῥώμην καὶ τὸν Ταρπήιον ὀνομάζοντες ἀεὶ λόφον καὶ τὸν ἐξηγητὴν ἀξιοῦντες μὴ σφετερίζεσθαι τὸ σημεῖον, ἀλλ' ἀπὸ τοῦ κρατίστου καὶ τοῦ δικαιοτάτου λέγειν. [2.] οὐ δυνηθεὶς δὲ παρακρούσασθαι τοὺς ἄνδρας ὁ μάντις οὐδὲ σφετερίσασθαι τὸν οἰωνὸν λέγει πρὸς αὐτούς, " Ἄνδρες Ῥωμαῖοι, λέγετε πρὸς τοὺς ἑαυτῶν πολίτας ὅτι κεφαλὴν εἵμαρται γενέσθαι συμπάσης Ἰταλίας τὸν τόπον τοῦτον ἐν ᾧ τὴν κεφαλὴν εὕρετε." ἐξ ἐκείνου καλεῖται τοῦ χρόνου Καπιτωλῖνος ὁ λόφος[1] ἐπὶ τῆς εὑρεθείσης ἐν αὐτῷ κεφαλῆς· κάπιτα γὰρ οἱ Ῥωμαῖοι καλοῦσι τὰς κεφαλάς.
3. Similarly, an augural report (by the assistant) was valid even if faked and even

if he reported signs that had never appeared: Livy, 10.40.11; Cicero, *Philippicae* 2.83; 2.89; 3.9; cf. Linderski, "The Augural Law," in *Aufstieg und Niedergang der römischen Welt* 2.16.3, ed. H. Temporini and W. Haase, pp. 2146ff., at pp. 2207, 2214.

4. For the form of prayer and of sacrifice, see, e.g., Wissowa, *Religion und Kultus*, pp. 396ff.; Latte, *Religionsgeschichte*, pp. 206ff., 209ff. For correctness in approaching a deity, see Wardman, *Religion*, pp. 7ff. For respect of *formulae* and the speaking of the correct words, see A. Momigliano, *C.A.H.* 7.2, p. 108, and J. A. North, *C.A.H.* 7.2, pp. 592f.

5. Pliny, *Historia naturalis* 28.3.10: "Quippe victimas caedi sine precatione non videtur referre aut deos rite consuli. [11.] Praeterea alia sunt verba inpetritis, alia depulsoriis, alia commendationis, videmusque certis precationibus obsecrasse summos magistratus et, ne quod verborum praetereatur aut praeposterum dicatur, de scripto praeire aliquem rursusque alium custodem dari qui adtendat, alium vero praeponi qui favere linguis iubeat, tibicinem canere, ne quid aliud exaudiatur."

6. For the creative power of the religious formula, see, e.g., T. Köves-Zulauf, *Reden und Schweigen: Römische Religion bei Plinius Maior* (Munich, 1972).

7. Cicero, *De harispicum responsis* 11.23: "An si ludius constitit aut tibicen repente conticuit aut puer ille patrimus et matrimus si tensam non tenuit, si lorum omisit, aut si aedilis verbo aut simpuvio aberravit, ludi sunt non rite facti, eaque errata expiantur et mentes deorum immortalium ludorum instauratione placantur." Cf. Latte, *Religionsgeschichte*, p. 24.

8. See also, e.g., Augustine, *De civitate Dei* 4.26. Cf. Latte, *Religionsgeschichte*, pp. 198f., 392f. For the social importance of rites in religion, see also A. R. Radcliffe-Brown, *Structure and Function in Primitive Society* (London, 1952), pp. 153ff.

9. I wish to distinguish requirements of form from requirements of formalities. Requirements of formalities involve an unnecessary step that is not inherent in its factual creation. Thus, the contract of deposit that came into being only when the object was delivered to the depositee involves a requirement of form, but not of formalities. But the verbal contract of *stipulatio* that required, for validity of the promise, the promisor to use the same verb as the preceding question involves formalities. For an extreme view on formalism and magic in very early Roman law, see A. Hagerström, *Der römische Obligationsbegriff*, vols. 1 and 2 (Uppsala, 1927, 1941), and *Der magistratische Ius in seinem Zusammenhang mit dem römischen Sakralrecht* (Uppsala, 1929). Cf. G. MacCormack, "Haegerstroem's Magical Interpretation of Roman Law," *Irish Jurist* 4 (1969): 153ff.

10. *G.* 3.92ff.

11. *G.* 3.93.

12. See A. Watson, "Artificiality, Reality, and Roman Contract Law," *T.v.R.* 57 (1989): 147ff., at pp. 150f. In that paper I stressed that the formalities separated *stipulatio* from the numerous instances where one person does something for another without wishing a specific obligation to be imposed on the latter.

13. See, e.g., A. Ernout and A. Meillet, *Dictionnaire étymologique de la langue latine* (Paris, 1979), p. 644; A. Walde and J. B. Hofmann, *Lateinisches Etymologisches Wörterbuch*, 5th ed. (Heidelberg, 1982), p. 579; Kaser, *Privatrecht* 1:168ff.

14. I have argued elsewhere that the real point of the *stipulatio* is nonetheless to give effect to the intention of the parties. Above all, they want the promise to be binding ("Artificiality," pp. 150f.). This argument is not excluded by an origin in religion.

15. See, e.g., A. Watson, *Roman Private Law Around 200 B.C.* (Edinburgh, 1971), pp. 129ff.; *Evolution of Law*, pp. 12ff.

16. Cicero, *De natura deorum* 3.30.74.

17. *D.* 4.3.1.1; cf. Lenel, *Edictum*, pp. 144ff.

18. *D.* 4.3.1.1. See A. Watson, "*Actio de dolo* and *actiones in factum*," *ZSS* 78 (1961): 392ff., at 401.

19. "Si in ea re nihil dolo malo Auli Agerii factum sit neque fiat" (*G.* 4.119; *D.* 2.24.10.2).

20. See, e.g., Thomas, *Textbook*, pp. 104ff.

21. See, e.g., A. Watson, *The Law of Obligations in the Later Roman Republic* (Oxford, 1965), pp. 257f.; Kaser, *Privatrecht* 1:244f.

22. In the present context we need not consider whether (as I believe) any verb could be used in classical law or (as B. Nicholas insists) there was a closed list of six verbs: for literature see Watson, *Law of Obligations*, p. 1 n. 6. Plautus, *Bacchides*, lines 880ff., shows that by the beginning of the second century B.C. a verb as general in its import as *dare*, "to give," could be used to make an enforceable *stipulatio*. Nicholas's objection, "Since Latin has no word for 'Yes,' the occurrence of, e.g., '*Dabis?*' '*Dabo*' in Plautus is no evidence for the admissibility of stipulations in this form at this time" (Jolowicz and Nicholas, *Introduction*, p. 279 n. 7), misses the point. It is not just that to *Dabis?* (will you give?), the reply is *Dabo* (I will give). The context shows that in the play an enforceable contract is precisely what is wanted. Thus at line 881, Chrysalus says to Cleomachus, "Demand from him" (that is, from Nicobulus), and to Nicobulus he says, "You, promise him." Nicobulus says, "I promise. Make your demand." Then Cleomachus, "Will you give me two hundred good gold pieces?" Chrysalus, "Say 'they will be given.' Reply." Nicobulus, "I will give." The legal import of what is going on is stressed.

23. See Ernout and Meillet, *Dictionnaire*, p. 644, s.v. *Spondeo*.

24. *G.* 2.14aff.

25. Though *in iure cessio*, a fictitious court procedure, could be used (*G.* 2.24ff.).

26. *G.* 1.119ff.

27. "Hunc ego hominem meum esse aio isque mihi emptus esto hoc aere aeneaque libra." On the meaning of this see A. Prichard, "Terminology in *Manicipatio*," *LQR* 76 (1960): 412ff.

28. For all of this, see A. Watson, *Failures of the Legal Imagination* (Philadelphia, 1988), pp. 88ff.

29. *G*. 2.104; see Watson, *Failures*, pp. 91f.

30. See, e.g., C. F. Kolbert and N. A. M. MacKay, *History of Scots and English Land Law* (Berkhamsted, 1977), pp. 238ff.; S. F. C. Milsom, *Historical Foundations of the Common Law*, 2d ed. (London, 1981), pp. 104, 120; W. M. Gordon, *Scottish Land Law* (Edinburgh, 1989), p. 26.

31. For my views on the need for specific verbal formulations in wills, see A. Watson, *The Law of Succession in the Later Roman Republic* (Oxford, 1971), pp. 40f., 122ff.

32. *Religionsgeschichte*, p. 63. The provision of the Twelve Tables referred to dealt with *nexum* and *mancipatio;* see Watson, *XII Tables*, pp. 111ff., 144f. It has nothing to do with the proper use of a formal formulation.

33. *Privatrecht* 1:28; cf. now Mitchell, *Patricians and Plebeians*, p. 173.

34. *G*. 4.11: "Actiones quas in usu veteres habuerunt legis actiones appellabantur, vel ideo quod legibus proditae erant (quippe tunc edicta praetoris, quibus complures actiones introductae sunt, nondum in usu habebantur), vel ideo quia ipsarum legum verbis accommodatae erant, et ideo immutabiles proinde atque leges observabantur. unde eum qui de vitibus succisis ita egisset, ut in actione vites nominaret, responsum est rem perdidisse, quia debuisset arbores nominare, eo quod lex XII tabularum, ex qua de vitibus succisis actio competeret, generaliter de arboribus succisis loqueretur."

35. *G*. 4.30: "Sed istae omnes legis actiones paulatim in odium venerunt. namque ex nimia subtilitate veterum qui tunc iura condiderunt eo res perducta est, ut vel qui minimum errasset litem perderet."

36. "Texts and Interpretation," pp. 4f.

37. But Fritz Schulz, for example, would give greater importance to formalism in early Roman law (*Legal Science* [Oxford, 1946], pp. 24ff., 28f., 35).

38. *Privatrecht* 1:27f., 39ff; see also p. 31 for his claim that the freedom of the pontiffs to build law was restricted after the Twelve Tables were enacted because they were tied by the wording of the legislation.

39. See chap. 10.

Chapter 5. *Votum* and *Stipulatio*

1. For vows in general, see, e.g., Latte, *Religionsgeschichte*, pp. 46f.; for the kinship of biblical vows with law, see C. Carmichael, *Law and Narrative in the Bible* (Ithaca, N.Y., 1985), pp. 246ff.

2. Only one reference to it survives from the republic: Varro, *De lingua latina* 5.85. J. Linderski kindly tells me he believes the brotherhood survived; see his forthcoming review of I. Paladino, *Fratres Arvales* (Rome, 1989), in *Classical Philology*.

3. See especially Wissowa, *Religion und Kultus*, pp. 381ff., 562ff.; W. Eisenhut, "*Arvales fratres*," in *Der Kleine Pauly* 2:629ff.; I. Paladino, *Fratres*.

4. "Juppiter o[ptime] m[axime], si imp[erator] Titus Caesar Vespasianus

Aug[ustus] pontif[ex] max[imus] trib[unicia] potest[ate] pater patriae et Caesar divi f[ilius] Domitianus, quos nos sentimus dicere, vivent domusque eorum incolumis erit a[nte] d[iem] III non[as] Ian[uarias], quae proximae p[opulo] R[omano] Q[uiritium] rei p[ublicae] p[opuli] R[omani] Q[uiritium] *erunt, fuerint*, et eum diem eosque salvos servaveris ex periculis, si qua sunt *eruntve ante* eum diem, eventumque bonum ita uti nos sentimus dicere *dederis, eosque in eo statu* quo nunc sunt, aut eo meliore servaveris, ast tu *ea ita faxsis*, tunc tibi nomine collegi fratrum Arvalium bubus *auratis II vovemus esse futurum. Iuno regina, quae in verba Iovi o[ptimo] m[aximo] bubus* auratis II vovimus esse futurum, *quod hodie vovimus, ast tu ita faxsis, tunc* tibi in eadem verba *nomine collegi fratrum Arvalium vaccis auratis II vovemus* esse futurum. *Minerva cet. Salus publica cet.*" (*C.I.L.* 6:506, no. 2059). In the text the words in italics have been lost but can be reconstructed from this and other inscriptions of the Arval brotherhood. Square brackets indicate where abbreviations occurred in the inscription. See also *C.I.L.* 6:3278, n. 32363; cf. Valerius Maximus, 4.1.10.

5. Livy, 22.10:1 "His senatus consultis perfectis L. Cornelius Lentulus pontifex maximus consulente collegio praetore omnium primum populum consulendum de vere sacro censet: iniussu populi voveri non posse. [2.] Rogatus in haec verba populus: 'Velitis iubeatisne haec sic fieri? Si res publica populi Romani Quiritium ad quinquennium proximum sicut velim eam salvam, servata erit hisce duellis, quod duellum populo Romano cum Carthaginiensi est, quaeque duella cum Gallis sunt qui cis Alpes sunt, [3.] ratum donum duit populus Romanus Quiritium, quod ver attulerit ex suillo ovillo caprino bovillo grege, quaeque profana erunt, Iovi fieri, ex qua die senatus populusque iusserit. [4.] Qui faciet, quando volet quaque lege volet facito; quo modo faxit, probe factum esto. [5.] Si id moritur quod fieri oportebit, profanum esto neque scelus esto; si quis rumpet occidetve insciens, ne fraus esto; si quis clepsit, ne populo scelus esto neve cui cleptum erit; [6.] si atro die faxit insciens, probe factum esto; si nocte sive luce, si servus sive liber faxit, probe factum esto; si antidea quam senatus populusque iusserit fieri faxitur, eo populus solutus liber esto.' "

6. It should be noted that the latter could be uttered only by dictators and supreme commanders (Macrobius, *Saturnalia* 3.9.9).

7. *Saturnalia* 3.9.7: "Est autem carmen hujus modi quo di evocantur cum oppugnatione civitas cingitur: 'Si deus, si dea est, cui populus civitasque Carthaginiensis est in tutela, teque, maxime, ille qui urbis hujus populique tutelam recepisti, precor venerorque veniamque a vobis peto ut vos populum civitatemque Carthaginiensem deseratis, loca, templa, sacra urbemque eorum relinquatis, absque his abeatis; [8.] eique populo, civitati, metum, formidinem, oblivionem injiciatis, proditique Romam ad me meosque veniatis, nostraque vobis loca, templa, sacra, urbs acceptior probatiorque sit, mihique populoque Romano militibusque meis praepositi sitis ut sciamus intellegamusque. Si ita feceritis, voveo vobis templa ludosque facturum.' "

8. See, e.g., Wissowa, *Religion und Kultus*, pp. 381ff.

9. For all this see Watson, *Evolution of Law*, pp. 3ff.

10. See *D.* 19.4.
11. See Kunkel, *Herkunft*, pp. 244f.
12. *D.* 19.5.5.
13. A. Watson, "Artificiality, Reality and Roman Contract Law," 57 *T.v.R.* (1989), pp. 147ff.
14. It is also precisely the form of the *lex* imposed by Priapus on the youth in *Carmina Priapea*, poem 5.
15. " 'Bene sponsis, beneque volueris' in precatione augurali Messalla augur ait significare spoponderis, volueris," cf. Latte, *Religionsgeschichte*, p. 67n.1.
16. At least in theory; the practice may have been different. See, e.g., Thomas, *Textbook*, pp. 201f.
17. For this development, see Watson, *Evolution of Law*, pp. 33ff.
18. But for religion, not just for *vota*; see the sources cited by Latte, *Religionsgeschichte*, p. 62.
19. *De legibus* 2.16.41.
20. *Saturnalia* 3.6.6; see also *D.* 50.12.2 (Ulpian); cf. Latte, *Religionsgeschichte*, p. 46.
21. See, e.g., *D.* 45.2.1; 9.2.54; 31.77.6; 46.1.21.5. There are echoes in a *votum* of other private-law institutions. Thus, *ne fraus esto* (let it be free from fraud) in Livy, 22.10.5, is reminiscent of *se fraude esto* (let it be without fraud) in Tab. 3.6. of the Twelve Tables.
22. See Watson, *Evolution of Law*, pp. 12ff.
23. See, e.g., on prayers, Cato, *De agri cultura* 132, 139, 140, 141; on sacrifices, Cato, *De agri cultura* 141, and Livy, 1.24ff.; on treaties, Livy, 1.24ff., 1.32.

Chapter 6. The Oath in Private Law

1. See, e.g., Kaser, *Zivilprozessrecht*, p. 60.
2. Or of 50 asses if the matter disputed was less than 1,000 asses; *G.* 4.16.
3. Neither of the words *vindicta* or *festuca* has any linguistic connection with any word denoting a spear; A. Walde and J. B. Hofmann, *Lateinisches Etymologisches Wörterbuch*, (Heidelberg, 1982), 1:489, 2:793.
4. See J. G. Wolf, "Zur *legis actio sacramento in rem*," in *Römisches Recht in der europäischen Tradition*, ed. O. Behrends, M. Diesselhorst, and W. E. Voss (Ebelsbach, 1985), pp. 1ff., at pp. 16ff. Against Wolf's claim that the *legis actio sacramento in rem* was originally designed for a claim of a slave, see A. Watson, *Slave Law in the Americas* (Athens, Ga., 1989), p. 139 n. 2.
5. See, e.g., Thomas, *Textbook*, p. 76.
6. It is of no consequence here whether the amount of the *sacramentum* was originally deposited in the public treasury or with the pontiffs. *G.* 4.16 mentions only the public treasury, but Varro, *De lingua latina* 5.180, says the money went *ad pontes*, "to

the bridges," which is probably a scribal error for *ad pontifices*, "to the pontiffs." There is no doubt that the pontiffs would be involved with the action, as they were concerned with interpretation, and the fate of the money deposited does not affect the very secular use of the *sacramentum*.

7. For this, see R. Bartlett, *Trial by Fire and Ordeal* (Oxford, 1986).

8. See, e.g., Kaser, *Zivilprozessrecht*, pp. 61f.; Wieacker, *Rechtsgeschichte* 1:273.

9. The existence of such a forerunner would, however, explain an apparent illogicality in the *legis actio sacramento*. Except for the exceptional (and explicable) case of *iusiurandum liberti*, an oath could not in Roman law validate the initiation of legal proceedings. How, then, could legal proceedings be begun without any apparent validation, and then progress on validation by an oath? That difficulty would disappear if the procedure was at first established for particular situations and involved religious connotations, but came to be used, almost surreptitiously, to bring in remedies for other situations. But to develop the law, dodges are frequently used even though they involve illogicalities; see, e.g., A. Watson, "Illogicality in Roman Law," *Israel Law Review* 1972:14ff.; D. Daube, "Fraud No. 3," in *The Legal Mind*, ed. N. MacCormick and P. Birks (Oxford, 1988), at pp. 1ff.

10. *G.* 2.96; cf. *Gai Epitome* 2.9.4.

11. See, e.g., D. Daube, "Actions between *Paterfamilias* and *Filiusfamilias* with *Peculium Castrense*," *Studi in memoria di Emilio Albertario* (Milan, 1950), 1:445ff. The general problem, too, that obligations were generally extinguished by change of status (*capitis deminutio*) should be noticed but need not detain us.

12. *G.* 2.96; *Gai Epitome*, 2.9.4; *D.* 40.12.44pr.

13. Mommsen suggests a scribal error: "a slave or only a freedman" (*utrum servus an dumtaxat libertus*): *The Digest of Justinian*, ed. T. Mommsen, P. Krueger, and A. Watson (Philadelphia, 1985), 4.83.

14. *D.* 40.12.44pr. (*Actions*, book 7): "Licet dubitatum antea fuit, utrum servus dumtaxat an libertus iurando patrono obligaretur in his quae libertatis causa imponuntur, tamen verius est non aliter quam liberum obligari. ideo autem solet iusiurandum a servis exigere, ut hi religione adstricti, posteaquam suae potestatis esse coepissent, iurandi necessitatem haberent, dummodo in continenti, cum manumissus est, aut iuret aut promittat."

15. Cicero, *Ad Atticum* 7.2.8. In other regards the text is not too helpful. Cicero was upset by ungrateful freedmen, and he followed the example of Drusus (who was praetor between 120 and 115 B.C.), who simply denied manumission when freed slaves refused to repeat the oaths they had given. This does not prove that an action would lie as early as this on the *iusiurandum liberti*. It proves only that an owner who freed slaves would want the oath repeated on manumission. It also does not show that there was no way to compel the freedman to repeat the oath. Drusus's course of action may simply have pleased him more. Kaser takes the passage as showing that an edict of Drusus prevented

freedmen who refused to repeat the oath from bringing the action for freedom, *vindicatio in libertatem* (*Privatrecht* 1:300 n. 31).

16. These are set out by A. Watson, "*Iusiurandum in litem* in the *bonae fidei iudicia*," *T.v.R.* 34 (1966): 176ff., at 176.

17. See, e.g., W. W. Buckland, *Textbook of Roman Law*, 3d ed., ed. P. Stein (Cambridge, 1963), pp. 659f.

18. *D.* 12.3.2 (Paul, *Sabinus*, book 13): "Sive nostrum quid petamus sive ad exhibendum agatur, interdum quod intersit agentis solum aestimatur, veluti cum culpa non restituentis vel non exhibentis punitur: cum vero dolus aut contumacia non restituentis vel non exhibentis, quanti in litem iuraverit actor."

19. *D.* 12.3.5.3 (Marcian, *Rules*, book 4): "Sed in his omnibus ob dolum solum in litem iuratur, non etiam ob culpam: haec enim iudex aestimat."

20. *D.* 12.3.1 (Ulpian, *Sabinus*, book 51): "Rem in iudicio deductam non idcirco pluris esse opinamur, quia crescere condemnatio potest ex contumacia non restituentis per iusiurandum in litem: non enim res pluris fit per hoc, sed ex contumacia aestimatur ultra rei pretium." See also *D.* 4.3.18pr; 5.1.64pr; 12.3.3; 12.3.8.

21. *D.* 12.3.4.2 (Ulpian, *Edict*, book 36): "Iurare autem in infinitum licet. sed an iudex modum iureiurando statuere possit, ut intra certam quantitatem iuretur, ne arrepta occasione in immensum iuretur, quaero. et quidem in arbitrio esse iudicis deferre iusiurandum nec ne constat: an igitur qui possit iusiurandum non deferre, idem possit et taxationem iureiurando adicere, quaeritur: arbitrio tamen bonae fidei iudicis etiam hoc congruit." See also *D.* 4.3.18pr. and 12.3.5.1, 2.

22. *D.* 12.3.11 (Paul, *Replies*, book 3): "De periurio eius, qui ex necessitate iuris in litem iuravit, quaeri facile non solere."

23. *Classical Roman Law* (Oxford, 1951), p. 370.

24. We need not consider all the suggestions of interpolation in the texts. The texts are too consistent and internally coherent to render the idea of wholesale interpolation plausible. See the approach in Watson, "*Iusiurandum*."

25. For a similar statement, but made in a general context, see Liebeschuetz, *Continuity*, p. 21. One might compare the approach using the *iusiurandum in litem* to the proposition stated by Daniel, J., in the North Carolina case of *Murphy v. Moore*, 4 *Iredell Equity* (1845), pp. 188, at p. 124. He claimed that in actions for detinue of slaves "juries often and properly find" the value of slaves to be higher than the true value "in order to enforce the delivery of the slaves, yet that is not the course, where it is known that the defendant cannot discharge himself by a delivery, as if the negro be dead, or is owned by another person."

26. *D.* 12.2.34.6, 7. In general see the texts in *D.* 12.2; cf. Buckland, *Textbook*, p. 633. The oath could even be used by agreement between the parties, outside of court proceedings.

27. *D.* 12.2.1.

28. *D.* 12.2.13.6.

29. I have long suspected that my conception of "second best and the law" (on which I have worked extensively but not published) is borrowed from my master, David Daube, but I cannot find it in his writings. The expert on Daube's oeuvre, Calum Carmichael, points me to D. Daube, "Some Forms of Old Testament Legislation," *Proceedings of Oxford Society of Historical Theology*, 1945: 36ff.; "Concessions to Sinfulness in Jewish Law," *Journal of Jewish Studies* 10 (1959): 1ff.; "Biblical Landmarks in the Struggle for Women's Rights," *Juridical Review*, 1978:177ff. But the notion there is not quite the one I am putting forward. Perhaps I am borrowing from a point made in conversation.

Chapter 7. The Pontiffs and the Family

1. For more detail see Watson, *XII Tables*, pp. 9ff.

2. The ceremony of *confarreatio* contained customary elements as well as legal requirements, and these may not always be distinguishable. That need not disturb us, since our principal concern is simply the central legal requirement of the intervention of the main priests. Mitchell claims *confarreatio* was restricted to the marriage of priests; *Patricians and Plebeians*, pp. 83f.

3. The sources on *confarreatio* are numerous: *G.* 1.112; *Epitome Ulpiani* 9.1; Servius, *In Verg. Georg.* 1.31 and *In Aen.* 4.103, 339, 374.

4. Not until the *lex Ogulnia* of 300 B.C. could plebeians be pontiffs.

5. See J. Linderski, "Religious Aspects of the Conflicts of the Orders: The Case of *Confarreatio*," in *Social Struggles in Archaic Rome*, ed. K. A. Raaflaub (Berkeley, 1986), pp. 244ff., at p. 246.

6. *G.* 1.112.

7. *G.* 1.110 and Boethius, *II ad top. Cic.* 3.14, have *farreo;* Arnobius, *Adversus gentes* 4.20, and Servius, *In Verg. Georg.* 1.31, have *farre.*

8. For the argument see Watson, *XII Tables*, pp. 9ff.

9. See chap. 2, n. 1.

10. For the argument see A. Watson, *The Law of Persons in the Later Roman Republic* (Oxford, 1967), pp. 19ff.

11. Possibly this conclusion is not correct, since in the absence of the flamen Dialis his ceremonies were performed by pontiffs.

12. For more detail, especially on my views, see Watson, *XII Tables*, pp. 40ff. There I suggested that, in early law, males who were *alieni iuris* could also be adrogated. I still hold to that belief, but it need not detain us in the present context.

13. One might compare English divorces before 1857, which could be granted only by act of Parliament and hence were restricted to the wealthiest segments of the community.

14. *G.* 2.101–103; *Epitome Ulpiani* 20.2; Aulus Gellius, *Noctes Atticae* 15.27.3; *J.* 2.10.1; Theophilus, *Paraphrasis* 2.10.1.

15. See, above all, Kaser, *Privatrecht* 1:125f.
16. For the argument see Watson, *XII Tables*, pp. 52ff.
17. Varro, *De re rustica* 2.4.9; Servius, *In Aen.* 3.136; 4.346.
18. Naturally, one could not expect the pontiffs to be directly involved. But the College of Pontiffs never established a hierarchy with the pontiffs akin to bishops, supported by the equivalent of parish priests and curates.

Chapter 8. Religion and Property

1. *G.* 2.2: "Summa itaque rerum divisio in duos articulos diducitur: nam aliae sunt divini iuris, aliae humani. [3] Divini iuris sunt veluti res sacrae et religiosae. [4] Sacrae sunt quae diis superis consecratae sunt, religiosae quae diis Manibus relictae sunt."

2. *De domo* 49.127: "Video enim esse legem veterem tribuniciam quae vetet iniussu plebis aedes, terram, aram consecrari." See also 50.128. Cf. Rotondi, *Leges publicae*, pp. 234.

3. Livy, 9.46.7: "Itaque ex auctoritate senatus latum ad populum est ne quis templum aramve iniussu senatus aut tribunorum plebei partis maioris dedicaret."

4. Livy, 9.46.6. Probably the issue was whether only magistrates *cum imperio* could dedicate a temple.

5. *Ad Atticum* 4.2.3.
6. *G.* 2.5.
7. *D.* 1.8.9.1.
8. See, e.g., *D.* 1.8.6.3.
9. Cicero, *De harispicum responso* 14.32.
10. Cicero, *De inventione* 1.8.11; 2.18.55; cf. Watson, *Law of Obligations*, pp. 226f.
11. See, e.g., Wissowa, *Religion und Kultus*, p. 385. M. Crawford has recently stressed: "In the middle and late Republic, then, it appears that there were three kinds of *res*, sacred, public, and private: and that the more important boundary was in some contexts between the first two and the last, not between the first and the last two" ("*Aut Sacrom aut Poublicom*," in *New Perspectives in the Roman Law of Property*, ed. P. Birks [Oxford, 1989], pp. 93ff., at p. 95). His arguments are not helpful. To support the claim that in the republic the essential boundary was not between divine and human, he cites Cicero, *De domo* 48.127–53.137, which shows absolute public control of the boundary between public and sacred (p. 94). The argument is irrelevant: there was also absolute public control of the boundary between public and private, and between private and sacred. Nor can it surprise that the aediles, in charge of streets, were responsible for the repair of that half of a street which ran beside a sacred or public space: *lex Iulia municipalis*, 45 B.C. (Bruns, *Fontes*, pp. 102ff. [no. 18], lines 29–31 [cf. lines 56–61]). See Wissowa, *Religion und Kultus*, pp. 406f. Most temples had little wealth of their own; see, e.g., Wardman, *Religion*, pp. 15f. The provision of the *lex Tarentina* (of the time of Cicero; Bruns, *Fontes*, pp. 120ff. [no. 27], lines 36–38), allowing a magistrate

to spend money collected from fines on games or a monument for himself on public property shows again public control over the public and sacred, but it does not show that, as Crawford claims, coming closer to property law, the important boundary was not between the divine and human but between public and sacred on the one hand, and private on the other. The same argument applies against his deductions from the *lex Silia* in the *Fragmentum Tudertinum* (Bruns, *Fontes*, pp. 157f. [no. 32], lines 5f.).

Above all one cannot use *C.I.L.* 1, p. 410, nos. 402 and 403 as Crawford does. He regards the first of these—both are from the Latin colony of Venusia—as "the most remarkable text of all." The senators "declared it was either sacred or public" (*censuere aut sacrom aut poublicom ese*). Crawford comments: "The object in question is land: and what is certain is that in this particular case, once it had been established that it was not private, it did not matter whether it was sacred or public, although the two categories were in general clearly distinct" (p. 95). But on the facts of the case (which we do not have) and of that in inscription no. 403 (which might concern the same case), greater precision may have been unnecessary. Someone was, perhaps, claiming land, and the response was that he could not be the owner, since the land was either public or sacred. As Crawford says, once it was established that the land was not private, it did not matter whether it was public or sacred. This need not be because the concept of public land was close to that of sacred land.

12. Cicero, *De domo sua* 53.136: "Quid? cum Licinia, virgo Vestalis, summo loco nata, sanctissimo sacerdotio praedita, T. Flaminino Q. Metello consulibus aram et aediculam et pulvinar sub Saxo dedicasset, nonne eam rem ex auctoritate senatus ad hoc collegium Sex. Iulius praetor rettulit? cum P. Scaevola, pontifex maximus, pro collegio respondit, QUOD IN LOCO PUBLICO LICINIA, CAII FILIA, INIUSSU POPULI DEDICASSET, SACRUM NON VIDERIER."

13. See, in general, O. Robinson, "The Roman Law of Burial and Burial Grounds," *Irish Jurist* 10 (1975): 175ff.

14. *G.* 2.2: "Religiosum vero nostra voluntate facimus mortuum inferentes in locum nostrum, si modo eius mortui funus ad nos pertineat."

15. *D.* 10.3.6.6.

16. *De legibus* 2.23.58.

17. *D.* 11.3.2pr.

18. *De legibus* 2.22.57.

19. *D.* 11.7.36 (Pomponius, *Quintus Mucius*, book 26): "Cum loca capta sunt ab hostibus, omnia desinunt religiosa vel sacra esse, sicut homines liberi in servitutem perveniunt: quod si ab hac calamitate fuerint liberata, quasi quodam postliminio reversa pristino statui restituuntur."

20. See, e.g., Watson, *Law of Persons*, pp. 253ff.

Chapter 9. State Religion and Alien Religion

1. But *pietas* is a requirement for Cicero, *De legibus* 2.8.19.

2. For ancient views on the utility of religion, see, e.g., Wardman, *Religion*, pp. 52ff.

3. For manipulation see, e.g., Wardman, *Religion*, pp. 42ff.

4. An obvious example is the long toleration and even support of Judaism in Asia Minor; see above all Josephus, *Jewish Antiquities* 14.10; 14.12; 16.6; 19.5; 19.6; 20.1. The symbiosis of other gods is also noticeable in the depiction of local deities on Greek imperial coins; see, e.g., K. Harl, *Civic Coins and Civic Politics in the Roman East, A.D. 180–275* (Berkeley, 1987). See also, e.g., R. MacMullen, *Paganism in the Roman Empire* (New Haven, 1981), pp. 1ff.; S. L. Guterman, *Religious Toleration and Persecution in Ancient Rome* (London, 1951).

5. *De legibus* 2.8.19: "Ad divos adeunto caste, pietatem adhibento, opes amovento. qui secus faxit, deus ipse vindex erit.

"Separatim nemo habessit deos neve novos neve advenas nisi publice adscitos; privatim colunto, quos rite a patribus cultos acceperint. . . .

"Ritus familiae patrumque servanto.

"Divos et eos, qui caelestes semper habiti, colunto et ollos, quos endo caelo merita locaverint, Herculem, Liberum, Aesculapium, Castorem, Pollucem, Quirinum, ast olla, propter quae datur homini ascensus in caelum, Mentem, Virtutem, Pietatem, Fidem, Earumque laudum delubra sunto, ne uncula vitiorum.

"Sacra sollemnia obeunto."

6. See Wardman, *Religion*, pp. 14f.

7. See the range of meanings supported by texts in, e.g., *The Oxford Latin Dictionary* (Oxford, 1982), s.v. *pietas*.

8. *De inventione* 2.22.66; cf. 2.53.161. See also, e.g., H. Wagenvoort, *Pietas: Selected Studies in Roman Religion* (Leiden, 1980), pp. 1ff.

9. S.v. *Religiosi:* "Religiosi dicuntur, qui faciendarum praetermittendarumque rerum divinarum secundum morem civitatis dilectum habent, nec se superstitionibus implicant."

10. Livy, 4.30.9: "Nec corpora modo adfecta tabo, sed animos quoque multiplex religio et pleraque externa invasit, novos ritus sacrificandi vaticinando inferentibus in domos quibus quaestui sunt capti superstitione animi, [10.] donec publicus iam pudor ad primores civitatis pervenit, cernentes in omnibus vicis sacellisque peregrina atque insolita piacula pacis deum exposcendae. [11.] Datum inde negotium aedilibus, ut animadverterent ne qui nisi Romani di neu quo alio more quam patrio colerentur." Livy also states elsewhere that only the Roman gods protect Rome; see, e.g., 3.7.7f.; 5.16.11; 5.51.5.

11. J. Linderski has commented in a private communication on this bareness of the Roman state religion, to my benefit. He writes: "This again depends on the point of

view; the Roman state religion was not a religion in the Christian (or 'oriental') sense of the word; it was a means to ensure the prosperity of the *res publica;* hence it was akin to our science, and as barren or as rich as science is (only that it was—viewed from a modern perspective—science turned upside down)."

12. On the aediles see, e.g., Wieacker, *Rechtsgeschichte* 1:478ff.
13. Aulus Gellius, *Noctes Atticae* 1.12.18.
14. Livy, 25.1.
15. Livy, 25.1.11: "Ubi potentius iam esse id malum apparuit quam ut minores per magistratus sedaretur, M. Aemilio praetori [urb.] negotium ab senatu datum est ut eis religionibus populum liberaret. [12.] Is et in contione senatus consultum recitavit et edixit ut quicumque libros vaticinos precationesve aut artem sacrificandi conscriptam haberet eos libros omnes litterasque ad se ante calendas Apriles deferret neu quis in publico sacrove loco novo aut externo ritu sacrificaret."
16. Livy, 39.8-19; for religious aspects see Latte, *Religionsgeschichte,* pp. 270ff.
17. For the evidence from Plautus of Dionysian rites in Rome, see Latte, *Religionsgeschichte,* p. 270 n. 6. Livy, 39.8.3, 39.12.9. The mysteries were already known in Campania; cf. Latte, *Religionsgeschichte,* pp. 270f.
18. Livy, 39.14.6-8.
19. Livy, 39.15.2: "Nulli umquam contioni, Quirites, tam non solum apta sed etiam necessaria haec sollemnis deorum comprecatio fuit, quae vos admoneret hos esse deos, quos colere venerari precarique maiores vestri instituissent, [3.] non illos, qui pravis et externis religionibus captas mentes velut furialibus stimulis ad omne scelus et ad omnem libidinem agerent."
20. Livy, 39.16.9: "Iudicabant enim prudentissimi viri omnis divini humanique iuris nihil aeque dissolvendae religionis esse, quam ubi non patrio sed externo ritu sacrificaretur."
21. Bruns, *Fontes,* p. 164 (no. 36).
22. For a massively detailed account of the Bacchanalia, see J.-M. Pailler, *Bacchanalia: La Répression de 186 av. J.-C. à Rome et en Italie* (Rome, 1988), esp. pp. 151ff.
23. For the acceptance of foreign and new gods at Rome, see, e.g., Wardman, *Religion,* pp. 2ff., 34ff., 49f.
24. For the numerous sources see Latte, *Religionsgeschichte,* pp. 258ff.
25. For Roman eagerness to acquire new deities during the Carthaginian war, see the examples provided by Wardman, *Religion,* pp. 34ff.
26. Dionysius of Halicarnassus, 2.19.5.
27. Suetonius, *Divus Claudius* 25.5. Pliny the Elder claims it was in the principate of Tiberius that the Druids were swept away, and he stresses the evil nature of that religion (*Historia naturalis* 30.4.13).
28. All the more is this true since I have nothing new to say on the persecutions. The essentially correct view is that expressed by G. E. M. de Ste. Croix, "Why Were the Early Christians Persecuted?" *Past and Present* 26 (1963): 6ff.; "Why Were the

Early Christians Persecuted?—A Rejoinder," *Past and Present* 27 (1964): 28ff. (For this evaluation of de Ste. Croix's thesis, see also R. L. Fox, *Pagans and Christians* [London, 1986], p. 749.) The important ancient sources are cited by him. The literature is enormous but see also, e.g., W. H. C. Frend, *Martyrdom and Persecution in the Early Church* (New York, 1967); and esp. Fox, *Pagans*, pp. 419ff., and O. Robinson, "Law and Order—On the Margins of the Criminal Law," *ZSS* (forthcoming). The most lucid account of toleration of Jews when Christians were persecuted is Fox, *Pagans*, pp. 428ff.

29. De Ste. Croix emphasizes that the repression of Christianity was different from that of other cults, such as the Bacchanalia ("A Rejoinder," p. 31). That is correct, but the attitude of the government was consistent. The problem was that Christianity was a permanent, unequivocal, denial of the official religion. Of course, Christians need not always be sought out when they were few and times were peaceable. Hence Trajan's advice to Pliny not to seek out the Christians but to punish any brought before him when the charge was proven, and to allow a pardon to those who repented and prayed to the Roman gods (Pliny, *Epistulae* 10.97).

Chapter 10. The Pontiffs and Legal Development

1. See Schulz, *Legal Science*, pp. 6ff.
2. Thomas, *Textbook*, p. 4.
3. Livy, 10.6.
4. See, e.g., Kunkel, *Herkunft*, pp. 38ff.
5. See A. Watson, "Roman Law and Common Law: Two Patterns of Legal Development," *Loyola Law Review* 36 (1990): 247ff., at 259.
6. For a full discussion see A. Watson, book review, *Michigan Law Review* 85 (1987): 1071ff., at 1079ff.
7. For the relevant texts see J. A. Ankum, "*Utilitatis causa receptum*," in *Symbolae Juridicae et Historicae Martino David Dedicatae*, ed. J. A. Ankum, R. Feenstra, W. F. Leemans (Leiden, 1968), pp. 1ff.
8. "Si ancillas omnes et quod ex his natum erit testator legaverit, una mortua Servius partum eius negat deberi, quia accessionis loco legatus sit: quod falsum puto et nec verbis nec voluntati defuncti accommodata haec sententia est."
9. It may be noted in passing that the opinion is not beneficial to the slave child. He will now belong to the heir and be separated from the slave women who will have been rearing him from the death of his mother.
10. For more on the text see, e.g., Watson, *Law of Succession*, pp. 93ff.
11. "Dominus servo aureos quinque eius legaverat: 'heres meus Sticho servo meo, quem testamento liberum esse iussi, aureos quinque, quos in tabulis debeo, dato'. nihil servo legatum esse Namusa Servium respondisse scribit, quia dominus servo nihil

debere potuisset: ego puto secundum mentem testatoris naturale magis quam civile debitum spectandum esse, et eo iure utimur."

12. *D.* 33.4.6pr.

13. See Watson, *Law of Succession*, p. 92; F. Horak, *Rationes Decidendi* (Innsbruck, 1969), 1:105f.

14. "Mulier, quae viro suo ex dote promissam pecuniam debebat, virum heredem ita instituerat, si eam pecuniam, quam doti promisisset, neque petisset neque exegisset. puto, si vir denuntiasset ceteris heredibus per se non stare, quo minus acceptum faceret id quod ex dote sibi deberetur, statim eum heredem futurum. quod si solus heres institutus esset in tali condicione, nihilo minus puto statim eum heredem futurum, quia ἀδήνατος condicio pro non scripta accipienda est."

15. See on the text, e.g., Horak, *Rationes Decidendi* 1:125f.

16. "An ei qui in potestate sit eius quem heredem instituimus recte legemus, quaeritur. Servius recte legari putat, sed evanescere legatum si, quo tempore dies legatorum cedere solet, adhuc in potestate sit, ideoque, sive pure legatum sit et vivo testatore in potestate heredis esse desierit, sive sub condicione et ante condicionem id acciderit, deberi legatum. Sabinus et Cassius sub condicione recte legari, pure non recte, putant; licet enim vivo testatore possit desinere in potestate heredis esse, ideo tamen inutile legatum intellegi oportere, quia, quod nullas vires habiturum foret si statim post testamentum factum decessisset testator, hoc ideo valere, quia vitam longius traxerit, absurdum esset. sed diversae scholae auctores nec sub condicione recte legari, quia, quos in potestate habemus, eis non magis sub condicione quam pure debere possumus."

17. See, above all, *D.* 34.7.1pr.; cf. W. W. Buckland, *Textbook of Roman Law*, 3d ed., by P. Stein (Cambridge, 1963), p. 345; H. Hausmaninger, "Celsus und die *regula Catoniana*," *T.v.R.* 36 (1968): 469ff.

18. See, e.g., Watson, *Law of Succession*, p. 159, and the authors he cites; Horak, *Rationes Decidendi* 1:134ff.

19. But *res nec mancipi* should have been conveyed only if there had been physical delivery.

20. Horak argues that for the Sabinians, but not for the Proculians, the obligation in a conditional legacy begins only with the fulfillment of the condition (*Rationes Decidendi* 1:136 n. 22).

21. "Non sunt liberi, qui contra formam humani generis converso more procreantur: veluti si mulier monstrosum aliquid aut prodigiosum enixa sit. partus autem, qui membrorum humanorum officia ampliavit, aliquatenus videtur effectus et ideo inter liberos connumerabitur."

22. "Mulier si monstruosum aliquid aut prodigiosum enixa sit, nihil proficit: non sunt enim liberi, qui contra formam humani generis conuerso more procreantur." [4] Partum, qui membrorum humanorum officia duplicavit, quia hoc ratione aliquatenus videtur effectum, matri prodesse placuit.

23. Indeed, Paul's *Sententiae* 4.9.2 might even suggest that the *senatus consultum*

(or the statute of Augustus that it may have referred to) did not use the term "children" but "births."

24. There are a few, a very few, texts where a decision is expressly result oriented. They are so anomalous that they stick out. The best example known to me is in *D.* 43.23.2.

25. A particularly good instance is to be found in the texts on the *senatus consultum Silanianum* that are analyzed in A. Watson, *Slave Law in the Americas* (Athens, Ga., 1989), pp. 7ff. See also *D.* 4.4.9.4; discussed by A. Watson, *Roman Slave Law* (Baltimore, 1987), pp. 9f.

26. It will be apparent that my understanding of the similarities between sacred and private law is not that expressed by Schulz, *Legal Science*, pp. 11f.

27. *Epistulae ad familiares* 7.10.2.

28. When I discussed Livy, 31.9.8.

29. *De oratore* 3.33.133: "Equidem saepe hoc audivi de patre et de socero meo, nostros quoque homines qui excellere sapientiae gloria vellent omnia quae quidem tum haec civitas nosset solitos esse complecti. Meminerant illi Sex. Aelium; M'. vero Manilium nos etiam vidimus transverso ambulantem foro, quod erat insigne eum qui id faceret facere civibus omnibus consilii sui copiam; ad quos olim et ita ambulantes et in solio sedentes domi sic adibatur non solum ut de iure civili ad eos verum etiam de filia collocanda, de fundo emendo, de agro colendo, de omni denique aut officio aut negotio referretur."

30. *De oratore* 1.45.200: "Est enim sine dubio domus iurisconsulti totius oraculum civitatis. Testis est huiusce Q. Mucii ianua et vestibulum, quod in eius infirmissima valetudine, affectaque iam aetate, maxima quotidie frequentia civium, ac summorum hominum splendore celebratur."

31. See further, Watson, *Law Making*, pp. 104f.

32. On *subscriptiones*, see, e.g., Jolowicz and Nicholas, *Introduction*, p. 369.

33. See, e.g., Watson, *Law Making*, pp. 149f.; Wieacker, *Rechtsgeschichte* 1:499.

34. See, e.g., E. Chénon, *Histoire générale du Droit français public et privé des Origines à 1815*, (Paris, 1926), 1:492ff.; F. Tomás y Valiente, *Manual de historia de derecho español*, 4th ed. (Madrid, 1982), pp. 150f.; D. Werkmüller, *Ueber Aufkommen und Verbreitung der Weistümer* (Berlin, 1972).

35. See, e.g., S. F. C. M. Milsom, *Historical Foundations of the Common Law*, 2d ed. (Toronto, 1980), p. 1.

36. In my view this statement should be seriously qualified: custom is not easily found; different people act in different ways in the same society; an accepted rule of customary law may continue although patterns of behavior change; much customary law is actually borrowed (*Evolution of Law*, pp. 43ff.).

37. It is sufficient to call attention to the differences in the standard textbooks of Roman law and of other systems. For Roman law see, e.g., Kaser, *Privatrecht* 1 and Thomas, *Textbook*; for English law, Milsom, *Historical Foundations*; for Span-

ish law, A. Garcia-Gallo, *Manual de historia del derecho español*, vol. 1, 10th ed. (Madrid, 1984).

38. See, e.g., Watson, *Slave Law in the Americas*, pp. 1ff.

Chapter 11. The Paradox Resolved

1. Livy, 3.34.6. Some modern scholars also seem to be misled; e.g., M. Cary and H. H. Scullard state: "The code of the 'Twelve Tables' was a comprehensive document, embracing both public and private life" (*A History of Rome*, 3d ed. [London, 1975], p. 67).

2. See, e.g., Latte, *Religionsgeschichte*, p. 64; M. Kaser, *Römisches Privatrecht*, 15th ed. (Munich, 1989), p. 17.

3. Cicero, *De re publica*, 2.37.63; Dionysius of Halicarnassus, 10.60.5; Livy, 4.1.1, 2; 4.2.6; 4.4.5–12; 4.5.5; 4.6.2. Cf. Watson, *XII Tables*, pp. 20ff.; J. Linderski, "Religious Aspects of the Conflict of the Orders: The Case of *confarreatio*," in *Social Struggles in Archaic Rome*, ed. K. A. Raaflaub (Berkeley, 1986), pp. 244ff., at pp. 252f. For the reasoning behind the prohibition, see J. Linderski, "The Auspices and the Struggle of the Orders," in *Staat und Staatlichkeit in der frühen römischen Republik*, ed. W. Eder (Stuttgart, 1990), pp. 34ff.

4. Linderski stresses that *confarreatio* at the time of the Twelve Tables was "a class institution and an instrument of class policy" ("Religious Aspects," p. 251).

5. Dionysius of Halicarnassus, 2.9.1f.

6. Dionysius of Halicarnassus, 2.10.1–3.

7. Tab. 8.21: "Patronus si clienti fraudem fecerit, sacer esto"; see Bruns, *Fontes*, p. 33.

8. See Watson, *XII Tables*, pp. 101ff.

9. Tab. 1.4: "Assiduus vindex assiduus esto; proletario [iam civi] quis volet vindex esto" (Aulus Gellius, *Noctes Atticae* 16.10.15).

10. See Festus, s.v. *vindex*. See, e.g., D. 2.4.22.1; cf. Kaser, *Zivilprozessrecht*, pp. 49ff.

11. See Festus, s.v. *adsiduus;* Nonius, s.v. *proletari;* cf. A. Neumann, s.v. *Proletarii* in *Der Kleine Pauly* 4.

12. See, e.g., Rotondi, *Leges publicae*, p. 236.

13. The chronology is doubted; see, e.g., Talamanca, *Lineamenti*, pp. 122ff.

14. Livy, 6.34–42; Dionysius of Halicarnassus, 4.62.4; cf., e.g., Wissowa, *Religion und Kultus*, p. 535.

15. Livy, 4.7.2; 5.12.9; see, e.g., A. Drummond, *C.A.H.* 7.2, pp. 192ff.

16. Livy, 6.42.9–11; 8.15.9; see, e.g., Mommsen, *Römisches Staatsrecht* Vol. 2 (Leipzig, 1887), p. 204.

17. Livy, 1.43.1–9; Dionysius of Halicarnassus, 4.16–18.
18. See, e.g., Wieacker, *Rechtsgeschichte* 1:392ff.; Talamanca, *Lineamenti*, pp. 63ff. The overall picture is not accepted by Mitchell, *Patricians and Plebeians*, pp. 53ff.
19. Livy, 1.43.9: "Haec omnia in dites a pauperibus inclinata onera. [10.] Deinde est honos additus; non enim, ut ab Romulo traditum ceteri servaverant reges, viritim suffragium eadem vi eodemque iure promisce omnibus datum est, sed gradus facti, ut neque exclusus quisquam suffragio videretur et vis omnis penes primores civitatis esset. [11.] Equites enim vocabantur primi; octoginta inde primae classis centuriae; ibi si variaret, quod raro incidebat, institutum ut secundae classis vocarentur, nec fere unquam infra ita descenderunt, ut ad infimos pervenirent."
20. C. Nicolet properly stresses that the highest classes bore a disproportionately great military and financial burden (*World of the Citizen*, pp. 49ff.).
21. We need not here discuss subsequent modifications that reduced the inequalities, but see Wieacker, *Rechtsgeschichte* 1:390ff. Nor need we discuss the *comitia tributa*, which had lesser but similar legislative powers and could be summoned only by the so-called patrician magistrates, the consuls (and after their creation in 367 B.C., also the praetors), but see Wieacker, *Rechtsgeschichte* 1:400ff.; Nicolet, *World of the Citizen*, pp. 225ff. Likewise we can omit the vexed question as to when *plebiscita* first became binding on patricians; see Wieacker, *Rechtsgeschichte* 1:403f.
22. For sources see Rotondi, *Leges publicae*, pp. 313f.
23. *World of the Citizen*, p. 5. We need not discuss subsequent changes in the appointment of judges.
24. See, e.g., Kunkel, *Herkunft*, pp. 50ff.
25. In this regard Roman law is markedly different from many other legal systems in which, for example, the penalty for wrongdoing varies according to the status of the victim. A prime example where private-law rights vary according to status is the Code of Hammurabi, who ruled in Babylon from about 1728 to 1686 B.C.: the best edition is *The Babylonian Laws*, 2 vols., ed. G. R. Driver and J. C. Miles (Oxford, 1952, 1955).
26. But the observance of its very strict forms could impart a sense of discipline; cf., e.g., Liebeschuetz, *Continuity*, pp. 6f.
27. See the sources cited by J. Marquardt, *Das Privatleben der Römer*, 2d ed. (Leipzig, 1886), 1:43 n. 12.
28. See the sources cited by Marquardt, *Privatleben* 1:47 nn. 3 to 8, 48 n. 1.
29. *De divinatione* 1.16.28.
30. See the sources cited by Marquardt, *Privatleben* 1:56 nn. 4–6.
31. Cicero, *De legibus* 2.20.49; 2.21.52; cf. Watson, *Law of Succession*, pp. 4ff.
32. Cicero, *De legibus* 2.19.48f.
33. *Captivi*, line 775; *Trinummus*, line 484; cf. Watson, *Law of Succession*, pp. 5f.
34. S.v. *sine sacris hereditas*.
35. See Kunkel, *Herkunft*, p. 12.

36. Cicero, *De legibus* 2.21.53; at 2.20.50 Cicero attributes the device to the Scaevolae.
37. *De legibus* 2.19.47.
38. *De legibus* 2.21.52.
39. Presumably by *legatum partitionis;* see Watson, *Law of Succession*, pp. 128f.
40. Varro, *De lingua latina* 6.29, 30, 53; Ovid, *Fasti* 1.47; Macrobius, 1.16.14; Suetonius in Priscian, 8.20 Keil; *G.* 4.29. I am completely convinced by the arguments of A. K. Michels that Varro (who has influenced the later writers) skews his definition by trying to link *dies fasti* with *fari*, "speak" (*Calendar*, pp. 48ff.). As she says, one must not see a survival of a primitive taboo in the fact that Varro emphasizes that the praetor must not, on *dies nefasti*, say the words *do, dico, addico* (*Calendar*, p. 48).
41. *De lingua latina* 6.30; quoted in chap. 1, above.
42. See Michels, *Calendar*, p. 115.
43. Cf. Michels, *Calendar*, pp. 53f.
44. See, e.g., Michels, *Calendar*, p. 29; Latte, *Religionsgeschichte*, p. 2.
45. See, e.g., Michels, *Calendar*, pp. 50ff.; Liebeschuetz, *Continuity*, p. 2.
46. See Michels, *Calendar*, pp. 48ff., 116. The adjectives *fastus* and *nefastus* are restricted in use to qualifying *dies;* see, e.g., Michels, *Calendar*, p. 48. This should not be thought to indicate that these days had more of a religious connection than had other days or other things. Rather, these days were official days that needed some designation and that chosen was the obvious.
47. Cicero, *Ad Atticum* 6.1.8: "E quibus unum ἱστορικὸν requiris de Cn. Flavio, Anni filio. Ille vero ante decemviros non fuit, quippe qui aedilis curulis fuerit, qui magistratus multis annis post decemviros institutus est. "Quid ergo profecit, quod protulit fastos?" Occultatam putant quodam tempore istam tabulam, ut dies agendi peterentur a paucis; nec vero pauci sunt auctores Cn. Flavium scribam fastos protulisse actionesque composuisse, ne me hoc vel potius Africanum (is enim loquitur) commentum putes." See also Cicero, *Pro Murena* 11.25.
48. Livy, 9.46.4: "Ceterum, id quod haud discrepat, contumacia adversus contemnentes humilitatem suam nobiles certavit; [5.] civile ius, repositum in penetralibus pontificum, evolgavit fastosque circa forum in albo proposuit, ut quando lege agi posset sciretur."
49. *D.* 1.1.2.7 (Pomponius, *Manual, sole book*): "Postea cum Appius Claudius proposuisset et ad formam redegisset has actiones, Gnaeus Flavius scriba eius libertini filius subreptum librum populo tradidit, et adeo gratum fuit id munus populo, ut tribunus plebis fieret et senator et aedilis curulis."
50. For the contrary opinion as to their accuracy, see, e.g., Schulz, *Legal Science*, pp. 9f. On Gnaeus Flavius see D. Daube, *Civil Disobedience in Antiquity* (Edinburgh, 1972), pp. 119ff., who rightly stresses the role of the patrician Appius Claudius.
51. *D.* 1.2.2.35 (*Manual, sole book*): "Iuris civilis scientiam plurimi et maximi viri professi sunt: sed qui eorum maximae dignationis apud populum Romanum fuerunt,

eorum in praesentia mentio habenda est, ut appareat, a quibus et qualibus haec iura orta et tradita sunt. et quidem ex omnibus, qui scientam nancti sunt, ante Tiberium Coruncanium publice professum neminem traditur: ceteri autem ad hunc vel in latenti ius civile retinere cogitabant solumque consultatoribus vacare potius quam discere volentibus se praestabant." On Coruncanius in general see F. D'Ippolito, *I Giuristi e la Città* (Naples, 1978), pp. 29ff.

52. There may also be significant corruption. Mommsen suggests that *solumque* should perhaps read *vel solebant* (*The Digest of Justinian*, ed. T. Mommsen, P. Krueger, and A. Watson [Philadelphia, 1985], 1:7 n. 8).

53. F. Schulz rejects the whole tradition given in the text (*Legal Science*, p. 10).

54. Basing himself on a different translation of *profiteri*, John Cairns takes the text as meaning that Coruncanius was the first to practice law publicly: "Tiberius Coruncanius and the Spread of Knowledge about Law in Early Rome," *Journal of Legal History* 5 (1984): 129ff. I prefer the meaning "to teach," but Cairns and I are in agreement in stressing the connection with Coruncanius being the first plebeian *pontifex maximus*.

55. *D.* 1.2.2.38 (*Manual, sole book*): "Sextum Aelium etiam Ennius laudavit et exstat illius liber qui inscribitur 'tripertita', qui liber veluti cunabula iuris continet: tripertita autem dicitur, quoniam lege duodecim tabularum praeposita iungitur interpretatio, deinde subtexitur legis actio." On Sextus Aelius in general see D'Ippolito, *Giuristi*, pp. 53ff.

56. *De legibus* 2.19.47: "Totumne? quid ita? quid enim ad pontificem de iure parietum aut aquarum aut ullo omnino nisi eo, quod cum religione coniunctum est? id autem quantulum est!"

57. For the argument see A. Watson, *The Making of the Civil Law* (Cambridge, Mass., 1981), pp. 14f.

Chapter 12. The *Leges Regiae*

1. But A. Momigliano accepts that the Roman kings made laws (*C.A.H.* 7.2, pp. 107f.).

2. Dionysius of Halicarnassus, 2.25.1. Of course, the husband or his paterfamilias was the owner of all the property.

3. Plutarch, *Romulus*, 22. There is an anachronism here in that Ceres was introduced only in 493 B.C.; cf. Latte, *Religionsgeschichte*, p. 161. For the history of the provision see A. Watson, "The Divorce of Carvilius Ruga," *T.v.R.* 33 (1965): 38ff.

4. Festus, s.v. *plorare*.

5. Dionysius of Halicarnassus, 2.15; 2.25.6; 2.26, 27. For the meaning of "selling" here see Watson, *XII Tables*, pp. 111ff.

6. Dionysius of Halicarnassus, 2.27.

7. Dionysius of Halicarnassus, 2.74.

8. Plutarch, *Numa*, 10.

9. Plutarch, *Numa*, 12.
10. Servius, *In Verg. Ecl.* 4.43.
11. Plutarch, *Numa*, 17.
12. *D.* 11.8.2.28; cf. E. Fraenkel, "Zum Texte römischer Juristen," *Hermes* 60 (1925): 415ff., at 426.
13. Dionysius of Halicarnassus, 3.23.
14. Dionysius of Halicarnassus, 4.25.
15. Festus, s.v. *Plorare*.
16. Dionysius of Halicarnassus, 2.9. The distinction between patrician and plebeian may only have hardened in the very early republic.
17. Dionysius of Halicarnassus, 2.10.
18. Dionysius of Halicarnassus, 2.12–14; 2.21, 22.
19. Pliny, *Historia naturalis* 32.2.20; Festus, s.v. *opima*.
20. Pliny, *Historia naturalis* 14.12.88. The latter should perhaps be regarded as sumptuary legislation.
21. Festus, s.v. *Paelices*.
22. Festus, s.v. *Occisum*.
23. Lydus, *De mensibus* 1.31.
24. Livy, 1.19.7.
25. Dionysius of Halicarnassus, 2.63–74.
26. See, e.g., Latte, *Religionsgeschichte*, pp. 121ff.
27. Cicero, *De re publica* 2.17.31.
28. Tacitus, *Annales* 12.8.
29. Livy, 1.32.5–14.
30. Dionysius of Halicarnassus, 4.25.2; Livy, 1.42.5–11.
31. "Roman Private Law and the *Leges Regiae*," *Journal of Roman Studies* 62 (1972): 100ff.
32. It should be observed that the rules of the laws of the kings, as they have come down to us, do not have the appearance of rules of customary law, though I lack the expertise to judge the impact of the transmission on the appearance of the regal rules. For the appearance of customary law see, e.g., J. A. Brutails, *La Coutume d'Andorre* (Paris, 1904); L. Schapera, *Handbook of Tswana Law and Custom*, 2d ed. (London, 1965); M. Gluckman, *The Judicial Process among the Barotse*, 2d ed. (Manchester, 1973).

Appendix

1. It is some indication of the accuracy of the historical tradition that Livy, who does not understand law—see, e.g., Watson, *XII Tables*, p. 171—but finds accounts of it in his sources, stresses that the plebs' demand was for equality of treatment, and this, in a topsy-turvy way, was precisely what was granted to them in the Twelve Tables.

2. The view is, of course, exaggerated; for juristic writings on public law see, e.g., Schulz, *Legal Science*, pp. 90, 138f.

3. See, e.g., Watson, *The Making of the Civil Law*, pp. 144ff.

4. "1.2.25. Alle wet is raeckende lands-stand, ofte byzonder burgerrecht.

"1.2.26. Wet raeckende lands-stand is, als van de godsdienst, van beleid van vrede ende van oorlog, van de hoogheid en de palen van't land, macht ende manier om wetten te maken ende voorrechten te vergunnen, macht om recht te spreecken van's lands goed; van de straffe der misdaden, met de ampten daer toe dienende."

5. "1.2.27. Wet raeckende bysonder burger-recht is sulcks als wy nu door sijn deelen sullen aenwijsen. Want hoewel de lands-stand raeckende wetten treffelicker ende ghewichtiger zijn, soo sal't nochtans beter zijn dat wy van't byzonder-burger-recht raeckende wetten eerst handelen, om dat het bysonder-recht ouder is als het ander dat lands-stand is raeckende."

6. Grotius claims he will deal with public law but never does (1.11.10; 1.14.6). On similar works see Watson, *The Making of the Civil Law*, pp. 63ff., 149.

7. Though, no doubt, practice was often different.

Index of Texts

A. NON-LEGAL SOURCES

1. Greek and Roman Writings

Arnobius
Adversus gentes
4.20	116n.7

Augustine
De civitate Dei
2.4	96n.9
4.8	95n.2
4.26	109n.8
4.27	101n.68

Boethius
II ad top. Cic.
3.14	116n.7

Carmina Priapea
5	113n.14

Cato
De agri cultura
132	113n.23
139	113n.23
140	113n.23
141	113n.23
146	79

Cicero
SPEECHES
Pro Caecina
19.54	102n.14

De domo sua
17.43	106n.28
48.127ff	117n.11
49.127	55; 117n.2
53.136	56; 118n.12

De haruspicum responsis
9.19	95n.2
11.23	109n.7
14.32	117n.9

Pro Murena
11.25	126n.47

Philippicae
2.32.80ff	100n.50
2.83	109n.3
2.89	109n.3
3.9	109n.3
11.8.18	97n.25

Pro Sestio
30.65	106n.28

LETTERS
Ad Atticum
4.2.3	55; 97n.32; 117n.5
4.2.23	97n.34
6.1.8	83; 126n.47
7.2.8	46; 114n.15

Ad familiares
7.10.2	70; 123n.27

PHILOSOPHICAL WRITINGS
Divinatio in Caecilium
5.18	104n.2; 107n.39

De divinatione
1.15.28	100n.49
1.16.28	125n.29
1.57.131	101n.59
1.58.132	13; 101n.58
2.24.51	101n.60
2.34.72f	100n.49
2.36.77	10; 99n.47

De legibus
1.21.55	102n.14
2.4.9	102n.21
2.7.15f	100n.50
2.8.19	59; 119n.1; 119n.5
2.12.31f	100n.50

Index

De legibus (continued)
2.16.41	113n.19
2.19.47	84; 126n.37; 127n.56
2.19.48f	125n.32
2.20.49	125n.31
2.20.50	126n.36
2.21.52	125n.31; 126n.38
2.21.53	126n.36
2.22.57	118n.18
2.23.58	118n.16
2.24.61	102n.14
3.4.11	106n.28
3.19.43	100n.50
3.19.44	106n.28

De natura deorum
2.3.8	95n.2
3.30.74	110n.16

De officiis
1.12.37	102n.14

De re publica
2.17.31	128n.27
2.36.61	106n.28
2.37.63	106n.6

RHETORICAL WRITINGS

De inventione
1.8.11	117n.10
2.18.55	117n.10
2.22.66	59; 119n.8
2.53.161	119n.8

De oratore
1.45.200	70; 133n.30
1.46.201	104n.2; 107n.39
3.33.133	70; 123n.29

Topica
4.23	102n.14

Dio Cassius
60.6.4	32

Dionysius of Halicarnassus
2.6	100n.50
2.9	128n.16
2.9.1f	124n.5
2.10	128n.17
2.10.1ff	124n.6
2.12ff	128n.18
2.15	127n.5
2.19.5	120n.26
2.21f	128n.18
2.25.1	127n.2
2.25.6	127n.5
2.26f	127n.5
2.27	127n.6
2.63ff	128n.25
2.74	127n.7
3.23	128n.13
4.16ff	125n.17
4.25	128n.14
4.25.2	128n.30
4.59	108n.1
4.60.1ff	30f; 108n.2
4.62.4	124n.14
6.17	96n.12
6.94.3	96n.12
10.1.1ff	23f; 105n.16
10.2.1	105n.17
10.3.3f	24; 105n.18
10.4	106n.19
10.31f	105n.14
10.51.5	24f; 106n.20
10.55.4ff	106n.21
10.57.6	106n.24
10.58.4	106n.23
10.60.5	102n.6; 124n.3

Festus
s.v. *Adsiduus*	124n.11
s.v. *Bene sponsis*	42; 113n.15
s.v. *Diffareatio*	102n.1
s.v. *Maximus pontifex*	97n.28
s.v. *Occisum*	128n.22
s.v. *Opima*	128n.19
s.v. *Paelices*	128n.21
s.v. *Plorare*	127n.4; 128n.15
s.v. *Religiosi*	60; 119n.9
s.v. *Sine sacris hereditas*	125n.34
s.v. *Vindex*	124n.10

Aulus Gellius

Noctes Atticae
1.12	59
1.12.18	120n.13
15.27.3	116n.14
16.10.15	124n.9

Josephus

Jewish Antiquities
14.10	119n.4
14.12	119n.4
16.6	119n.4
19.5	119n.5
19.6	119n.6
20.1	119n.6

Livy
1.19.4	100n.50
1.19.7	128n.24
1.24ff	113n.23
1.32	113n.23

Index

1.32.5ff	128n.29	27.25.7ff	7; 98n.36
1.42.5ff	128n.30	31.8.3	97n.34; 99n.41
1.43.1ff	125n.17	31.9.5ff	8; 98n.37
1.43.9ff	77; 125n.19	31.9.8	123n.28
3.7.7f	119n.10	34.44.2	97n.34; 99n.40
3.9.1ff	22; 103n.25; 104n.6	38.51.1ff	97n.25
3.10.5ff	104n.7	39.8ff	120n.16
3.11.3	104n.8	39.8.3	120n.17
3.11.9	104n.8	39.12.9	120n.17
3.11.12	104n.8	39.14.6ff	120n.18
3.11.13	104n.8	39.15.2f	61; 120n.19
3.15.1	104n.8	39.15.11	101n.65
3.18.6	104n.8	39.16.9	61
3.19.11	22; 104n.9		

Lydus

De mensibus

1.31	128n.23

3.31ff	105n.14		
3.31.5ff	104n.10		
3.32.1	104n.12		

Macrobius

Saturnalia

3.32.5ff	23; 104n.13	1.16.9ff	10f; 100n.52
3.34.6	106n.24; 124n.1	1.16.14	126n.40
4.1.1f	102n.6; 124n.3	1.16.25	8; 98n.39
4.2.6	124n.3	3.6.6	113n.20
4.3.17	106n.23	3.9.7	40; 112n.7
4.4.5ff	102n.6; 124n.3	3.9.9	112n.6
4.5.5	102n.6; 124n.3		
4.6.2	102n.6; 124n.3		

Nonius

4.7.2	124n.15		
4.7.3	101n.69	s.v. *Deivitant*	101n.61
4.30.9ff	60; 119n.10	s.v. *Proletari*	124n.11

Ovid

Fasti

5.12.9	124n.15		
5.16.11	119n.10		
5.17	101n.69	1.47	126n.40

Plautus

Asinaria

5.25.7	97n.34; 99n.40		
5.51.5	119n.10	259ff	101n.59

Bacchides

6.27.5	101n.69		
6.34ff	124n.14		
6.38.9f	101n.69	880ff	110n.22

Captivi

6.42.9ff	124n.16		
8.15.6	101n.69		
8.15.9	124n.16	775	125n.33

Mostellaria

8.17.4	101n.69		
8.23.14	97n.34; 99n.40	571	101n.59

Trinummus

8.29ff	101n.69		
9.7.13f	101n.69	484	125n.33

Pliny the Elder

Historia naturalis

9.46.4f	83; 126n.48		
9.46.6	117n.4		
9.46.7	55; 117n.3	8.77.206	99n.40
10.6	121n.3	14.12.88	128n.20
10.40.11	109n.3	18.41ff	103n.29
10.47.1	101n.69	28.3.10	31f; 100n.50; 109n.5
22.10.1ff	40; 112n.5	28.4.17	10; 100n.48
22.10.5	113n.21	30.4.13	120n.27
22.33.12	101n.69	32.2.20	128n.19
23.19.3	101n.69		
25.1	120n.14		
25.1.11f	60f; 120n.15		

Plutarch
  Lives
    Caesar
      7.29 — 101n.62
    Coriolanus
      25.3 — 32
    Numa
      10 — 127n.8
      12 — 128n.9
      17 — 128n.11
    Romulus
      22 — 127n.3
  Quaestiones Romanae
    50 — 102n.1
Polybius
  6.56.6ff — 95n.2; 100n.50
Priscian
  8.20 Keil — 126n.40
Sallust
  Bellum Catilinae
    12.3 — 95n.2
  Bellum Jugurthinum
    14.19 — 95n.2
Servius
  In Verg. Aen.
    3.136 — 117n.16
    4.103 — 116n.3
    4.339 — 116n.3
    4.346 — 117n.16
    4.374 — 116n.3
  In Verg. Eccl.
    4.43 — 128n.10

In Verg. Georg.
    1.31 — 116n.3; 116n.7
Suetonius
  Divus Claudius
    25.5 — 120n.27
  Divus Iulius
    13 — 101n.62
Tacitus
  Annales
    1.10 — 99n.41
    12.8 — 128n.28
Tertullian
  Apologeticus
    25.2 — 95n.2
Valerius Maximus
    1.1.8f — 95n.2
    4.1.10 — 112n.4
Varro
  De lingua latina
    5.85 — 111n.2
    5.180 — 113n.6
    6.29 — 126n.40
    6.30 — 11; 100n.53; 126n.40; 126n.41
    6.53 — 126n.40
  De re rustica
    2.4.9 — 117n.17

2. BIBLICAL TEXTS

Exodus
    20.12 — 103n.35
Numbers
    5.11ff — 49

B. LEGAL SOURCES

1. LAWS

Duodecim Tabulae
    1.4 — 75; 124n.9
    3.6 — 113n.21
    6.1 — 36
    8.1 — 103n.27; 103n.28
    8.8 — 103n.27; 103n.29
    8.9 — 103n.27; 103n.30
    8.10 — 103n.27
    8.14 — 103n.27
    8.15 — 103n.29
    8.21 — 74; 103n.27; 103n.31
    8.23 — 103n.27
    8.24 — 103n.32; 124n.7
    8.34 — 103n.27
    9.1 — 26
    9.2 — 26

9.3	103n.27	3.92ff	109n.10
9.4	103n.27	3.93	109n.11
9.5	103n.27	4.11	36; 111n.34
10	103n.27	4.13ff	44
12.4	103n.33	4.16	113n.2; 113n.6
		4.19	98n.38
		4.30	36; 111n.35
		4.119	110n.19

2. Inscriptions

Bruns *Fontes*

		Pauli Sententiae	
p. 8f	103n.23	4.9.2	122n.23
p. 33	124n.7	4.9.3f	69; 122n.22
p. 102ff	117n.11	*Ulpiani Epitome*	
p. 120ff	117n.11	2.4	102n.11
p. 157f	118n.11	9.1	116n.3
p. 164	120n.21	20.2	116n.14
p. 249	97n.31; 99n.40		
p. 283	100n.55		
p. 385f	99n.41		

4. Justinianian Works

C.I.L.

Digesta

1, no. 402 (at p. 410)	118n.11	1.1.1.2	101n.67; 107n.40
1, no. 403 (at p. 410)	118n.11	1.1.2.7	83; 126n.49
6.2, no. 10675	99n.41	1.1.7.1	107n.36
6.2059	39; 111n.4	1.1.10pr.ff	29; 107n.41
6.3278	112n.4	1.2.2.5f	16f; 107n.29
10.2, 985, no. 8259	8f; 97n.31; 99n.40	1.2.2.35	83; 126n.51
		1.2.2.38	84; 127n.55
		1.5.14	68; 122n.21
		1.8.6.3	117n.8
		1.8.9.1	117n.7

3. Pre-Justinianian Legal Writings

		2.4.22.1	124n.10
		2.24.10.2	110n.29
Gai Epitome		4.3.1.1	110n.17; 110n.18
2.9.4	114n.10; 114n.12	4.3.18pr	115n.21
Gaius		4.4.9.4	123n.25
Institutiones		9.2.54	113n.21
1.110	116n.6	10.3.6.6	118n.15
1.112	116n.3; 116n.7	11.3.2pr	118n.17
1.119ff	110n.26	11.7.36	57; 118n.19
1.144f	18; 103n.24	11.8.2.28	128n.12
2.2	56; 117n.1; 118n.14	12.2	115n.26
2.2ff	55	12.2.1	115n.27
2.5	117n.6	12.2.13.6	116n.28
2.14a.ff	110n.24	12.2.34.6f	115n.26
2.24ff	110n.25	12.3.1	47; 115n.20
2.42	102n.14	12.3.2	47; 115n.18
2.45	102n.14	12.3.3	115n.20
2.47	102n.14	12.3.4.2	47; 115n.21
2.49	102n.14	12.3.5.1f	115n.21
2.54	102n.14	12.3.5.3	47; 115n.19
2.96	114n.10; 114n.12	12.3.8	115n.20
2.101ff	116n.14	12.3.11	47; 115n.22
2.204	102n.14	19.4	113n.10
2.244	66; 122n.16	19.5.5	113n.12
		28.7.20pr	65f; 122n.14

Index

Digesta (continued)

30.63	65; 121n.8
31.77.6	113n.21
33.4.6pr	122n.12
34.7.1pr	122n.17
35.1.40.3	65; 121n.11
40.1.25	102n.11
40.1.29.1	102n.11
40.12.44pr	46; 114n.12; 114n.14
41.3.33pr	102n.14
43.23.2	123n.24
44.6.3	103n.33
45.2.1	113n.21
46.1.21.5	113n.21
50.12.2	113n.20

Institutiones

1.1pr	107n.41
1.1.1	107n.41
1.1.3	107n.41
1.1.4	107n.40
1.20.3	107n.34
2.6.2	102n.14
2.10.1	116n.14
4.10	103n.27

5. BYZANTINE WORKS

Theophilus

Paraphrasis

2.10.1	116n.14

www.ingramcontent.com/pod-product-compliance
Lightning Source LLC
Chambersburg PA
CBHW011232160426
43202CB00020B/2982